17,000
CLASSROOM VISITS
CAN'T BE WRONG

ASCD MEMBER BOOK

Many ASCD members received this book as a
member benefit upon its initial release.

Learn more at: **www.ascd.org/memberbooks**

17,000
CLASSROOM VISITS CAN'T BE WRONG

Strategies That Engage Students, Promote Active Learning, and Boost Achievement

John V. Antonetti
James R. Garver

ASCD

Alexandria, Virginia USA

1703 N. Beauregard St. • Alexandria, VA 22311-1714 USA
Phone: 800-933-2723 or 703-578-9600 • Fax: 703-575-5400
Website: www.ascd.org • E-mail: member@ascd.org
Author guidelines: www.ascd.org/write

Judy Seltz, *Executive Director;* Stefani Roth, *Publisher;* Genny Ostertag, *Director, Content Acquisitions;* Julie Houtz, *Director, Book Editing & Production;* Jamie Greene, *Editor;* Georgia Park, *Senior Graphic Designer;* Mike Kalyan, *Manager, Production Services;* Val Younkin, *Production Designer;* Kyle Steichen, *Production Specialist*

PAPERBACK ISBN: 978-1-4166-2008-2   ASCD product #115010

PDF E-BOOK ISBN: 978-1-4166-2043-3; see Books in Print for other formats.

Quantity discounts: 10–49, 10%; 50+, 15%; 1,000+, special discounts (e-mail programteam@ascd.org or call 800-933-2723, ext. 5773, or 703-575-5773). For desk copies, go to www.ascd.org/deskcopy.

ASCD Member Book No. F15-5 (Feb. 2015 P). ASCD Member Books mail to Premium (P), Select (S), and Institutional Plus (I+) members on this schedule: Jan, PSI+; Feb, P; Apr, PSI+; May, P; Jul, PSI+; Aug, P; Sep, PSI+; Nov, PSI+; Dec, P. For current details on membership, see www.ascd.org/membership.

Library of Congress Cataloging-in-Publication Data
Antonetti, John V.
    17,000 classroom visits can't be wrong : strategies that engage students, promote active learning, and boost achievement / John V. Antonetti & James R. Garver.
        pages cm
    Includes bibliographical references and index.
    ISBN 978-1-4166-2008-2 (pbk. : alk. paper) 1. Teaching. 2. Active learning. 3. Motivation in education. 4. Academic achievement. I. Garver, James R. II. Title.
    LB1025.3.A55 2004
    371.102—dc23
                                                                                        2014042384

23 22 21 20 19 18 17 16 15   2 3 4 5 6 7 8 9 10 11 12

17,000
CLASSROOM VISITS CAN'T BE WRONG
Strategies That Engage Students, Promote Active Learning, and Boost Achievement

One's mind, once stretched by a new idea, never regains its original dimensions.
—Oliver Wendell Holmes, Sr.

If we are not careful, teaching can become an isolated profession.

If we are lucky, we become part of a team that works together and shares best practices.

If we are truly blessed, we find colleagues who help us reflect on our practice, stretch our thinking and force us to recognize our weaknesses and refine our strengths.

This book is dedicated to coauthor Dr. James R. Garver, who worked tirelessly and courageously to see this manuscript finished. He will not be physically present as the book is published, but I can promise you that his words will live on to provide wisdom, humor, and a unique look at the students who enter our classrooms every day.

To Jim: my friend, mentor, business partner, and brother.

You will forever be my Colleague.
—John Antonetti

Okay, so I GET to write whatever I want. What if I don't want to write anything, because I don't. She says it doesn't matter what I write and that she won't get mad at anything I write. As long as I write MY thoughts. Its supposed to be about thinking.

Okay, so Daniella just asked how long it has to be. Mrs. Garcia said length is not a trait. What does that mean? Long or short? I can't believe I'm in the same class with Daniella for English and Social Studies. Double block. yuck!!!!! two hole hours together.

So for eight minutes every day we're going to write whatever we are thinking about. What I'm thinking about is how come seventh graders have to write a diary anyway?

Curtis says his English class doesn't have to do this. Who gets to decide this stuff anyway? If Mrs. Garcia says we have to but Ms. Miller's Kids don't have to, it's not fair. Nobody asked me!

Nobody ever asks Kids about how to run school and we're the only ones who have to come every day. It's not fair.

1 more minute to write. Right? Right! Write. write writewritewritewritewrite.

Mrs. Garcia, if you read this, you have to say I did it RIGHT, cuz I wrote about what I was thinking.

Focus on Learning

These frustrated ramblings in a 7th grader's journal are all too familiar to most educators. Teachers spend time planning lessons, basing them on standards and guided by curricula and instructional materials, only to be met with resistance and apathy. We try to keep up with developments in instruction—you wouldn't be reading this book if you didn't—but the pieces often seem to remain disparate and not come together. Perhaps it's a matter of changing our focus. Have we considered what our lessons might look like from the other side of the desk?

As the authors of this book, we have looked at instruction in more than 17,000 elementary and secondary classrooms. During this experience, we have come to recognize the power of shifting the focus from teaching to learning. This realization has come both over time and in a few blinding moments of clarity.

A few years ago, we hosted our first annual Engagement Conference in Las Vegas. On the eve of that conference, like expectant parents, we carefully reviewed our plans for the following days, ensuring that every detail was covered. Finally, at about 10:30 p.m., John said, "I think we're ready, but you don't seem very happy."

"What's the 'big idea' for our conference?" Jim asked.

"That kids need to be more engaged ... actively involved in learning activities."

"And how are we starting?"

"With your 90 minute keynote speech ..."

And at that point, we both realized that wouldn't work. So, we set about designing a new conference opening—one in which participants would be

3

physically and cognitively involved in the work. We were nervous, because we had never seen this kind of thing done in a large general session, but it gave rise to one of our favorite sayings: "Trust the learners."

A major purpose of this book is to help educators understand and develop this trust. Whether you are serving as a classroom teacher, site administrator, district leader, school board member, or parent, this idea can have powerful implications. In the following pages, we will share:

- What's really going on in classrooms around the country.
- Benchmarks to determine where your school is on the continuum of effective instruction.
- Good classroom practices for implementation and professional development.
- Tools and techniques to improve academic scores.
- Qualities that will result in students being more engaged.
- Strategies that develop higher-level thinking.
- Techniques to lead professional learning communities (PLCs) in a new, more thoughtful direction.
- A vision of what your school could be.

For many reasons—the movement to standards and accountability being chief among them—one might think that a shift toward learning-focused instruction should have already happened. Unfortunately, testing elevated the importance of results but not the learning process.

In a traditional classroom model, time is the constant and learning is the variable. That is, all students receive the same instruction for roughly the same amount of time. The results—not surprisingly—are a bell curve. Some students learn the content deeply and well, most have a moderate level of comprehension, and a few don't learn it at all. With the advent of standards, learning has become the desired constant, yet one of the most important variables—time—was never adjusted. Another element of the learning process resistant to change has been the traditional role of the teacher.

For more than 20 years, the International Association for the Evaluation of Educational Achievement has provided educators around the world with statistics regarding math and science achievement. In 1999, the Trends in International Mathematics and Science Study (TIMSS) analyzed math classes in seven nations to examine the relationship between the cognitive demands of mathematical tasks and student achievement. In this study, a random sample of 100 8th grade math classes from each of the countries (Australia, the Czech Republic, Hong Kong [China], Japan, the Netherlands, Switzerland, and the United States) was videotaped during the school year. The six other countries were selected because each performed significantly higher than the United States on the TIMSS 1995 mathematics achievement test for 8th grade (Stigler & Hiebert, 2004).

In the 1999 video study, the classroom math tasks were categorized as either *using procedures* (i.e., requiring basic computational skills and procedures) or *making connections* (i.e., focusing on concepts and connections among mathematical ideas). The problems were coded twice—once to characterize the type of math problem and once to describe its implementation in the classroom.

Figure 1.1 captures the percentage of each type of math problem presented in six of the seven countries.

Approximately 17 percent of the problem statements in the United States suggested a focus on mathematical connections or relationships. This percentage is within the range of several high-achieving countries (i.e., Hong Kong, Czech Republic, Australia).

As students worked through the math problems, the video study analyzed teacher-student interactions and the mathematical approach taken to solve the problems. Figure 1.2 shows the coding of the student work as it was actually performed by students.

Though the curriculum may have involved a balance in the types of problems proposed, virtually none of the *making connections* problems observed in the United States were implemented in a way that guaranteed conceptualization or demanded mathematical connections be made by students. There are a number of issues highlighted by the study, but the most troubling finding of all is that teachers in the United States reduced most problems to procedural exercises or simply gave students the answers—efficient teaching perhaps, but ineffectual learning.

If the TIMSS video study had only looked at instructional delivery or the resulting achievement measures, these issues might not have been as obvious. Focusing on students during academic activities provided the greatest clarity into the achievement results.

Why does this disconnect between curriculum and implementation occur in the United States? Math teachers across the country have shared with us many valid reasons when we ask this very question:

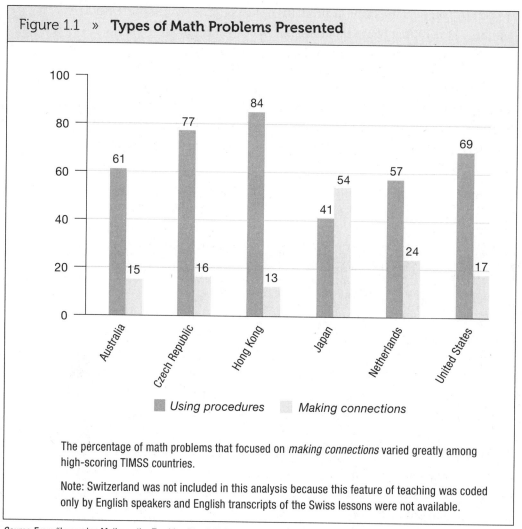

Figure 1.1 » Types of Math Problems Presented

The percentage of math problems that focused on *making connections* varied greatly among high-scoring TIMSS countries.

Note: Switzerland was not included in this analysis because this feature of teaching was coded only by English speakers and English transcripts of the Swiss lessons were not available.

Source: From "Improving Mathematics Teaching," by J. W. Stigler and J. Hiebert, 2004, *Educational Leadership, 61*(15), p. 14. Copyright 2004 by ASCD.

- "Our curriculum is too full, inviting coverage and speed over deep mathematical understanding."
- "The discomfort of letting our students struggle; the need to rescue our students and then move on."
- "The pressure of the ever-present high-stakes testing."

- "The fear that a visiting administrator who walks in during a moment of student struggle might not see the teacher 'teaching.'"
- "It takes too long for them to figure it out."

This challenge remains today. Math teacher Dan Meyer put it into perspective when he said that we are "taking a compelling question, a compelling answer... but we are paving a smooth, straight path between the two and congratulating our students for how well they can step over the cracks on the way" (Meyer, 2013).

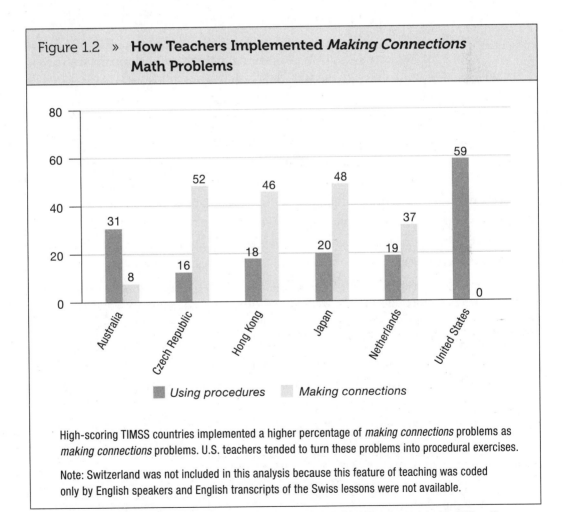

Figure 1.2 » **How Teachers Implemented** *Making Connections* **Math Problems**

High-scoring TIMSS countries implemented a higher percentage of *making connections* problems as *making connections* problems. U.S. teachers tended to turn these problems into procedural exercises.

Note: Switzerland was not included in this analysis because this feature of teaching was coded only by English speakers and English transcripts of the Swiss lessons were not available.

Source: From "Improving Mathematics Teaching," by J. W. Stigler and J. Hiebert, 2004, *Educational Leadership, 61*(5), p. 15. Copyright 2004 by ASCD.

Task predicts performance. —Richard Elmore

The idea of a teaching-learning shift didn't spring into our minds fully formed. As you may have already gleaned, we had the opportunity to examine teaching and learning in a variety of classroom situations—more than 17,000 and counting. We conducted the vast majority of those visits through the classroom walkthrough process. It was in that environment that we first worked together and that our ideas about the teaching-learning shift became concrete.

In 2001, we were asked by a professional development company to help create one of the first classroom walkthough models. It became very popular, and we helped train thousands of educators across North America. In 2005, we decided to form our own organization, Colleagues on Call. To begin this new venture, we asked ourselves what we learned about classroom walkthroughs.

The answer, unsurprisingly, came from the teachers with whom we worked. They said, "We know your visits aren't supposed to be evaluative, but sometimes it still feels like evaluation." It didn't take long to figure out why teachers felt that way: we were looking in the wrong place. Most of the data gathered and feedback provided were based on teachers' behaviors. When the focus of the visits was shifted to students, the differences were dramatic. Suddenly, we had a data set that could be gathered in no other way. Instead of monitoring whether an objective was posted on the board, students were asked to explain what they were learning and why it was relevant. In this way, thinking levels could be viewed across content areas and grade levels. Whereas formal assessments provided post-instructional data, observations made during these walkthroughs provided teachers with real-time data they could use to make instructional decisions.

We call this process Look 2 Learning (L2L), and if you glance at the contents for this book, you will get a fairly accurate picture of what we look for— from the students' point of view—during our classroom visits.

Here's how it works: After two days of training, L2L team members (alone or in pairs) visit classrooms in their respective schools for two to four minutes. While there, they listen to conversations and interactions, look at student work, and talk to students. Information is collected on an electronic device or on paper. Over time, the data are aggregated so trends and patterns can be observed. This information is then shared with classroom teachers, who— through reflective conversations—determine which professional practices they might like to refine. L2L data can then be used to monitor progress. Adjustments can be made and celebrations scheduled—all based, of course, on the learning and not the teaching.

Several times in this book, we will mention the use of continua. We think they can be powerful organizers for graphically representing complex relationships and relative magnitudes. For the present discussion, a continuum can help depict the teaching-learning shift and the change in focus that happens with Look 2 Learning walkthroughs.

In general, a continuum shows a relationship of degree that is indicated by position from left to right. It might look something like this:

weak, ineffective   strong, effective

We can also make use of the vertical dimension. For instance, a point high above the line could indicate a behavior solidly in adult control, whereas one below the line could denote a significant level of student control.

Adult Control

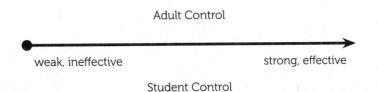

weak, ineffective   strong, effective

Student Control

Earlier, when we discussed the shift in focus brought about by Look 2 Learning walkthroughs, we mentioned learning objectives. Where on this continuum might we locate "The objective was written on the whiteboard"? First, think vertically; we can identify this as a behavior under the control of the adult, so it should appear above the line. Now we need to determine our position horizontally. Simply posting the objective isn't very effective in improving learning by itself. Therefore, the placement of this task on the continuum might look like this:

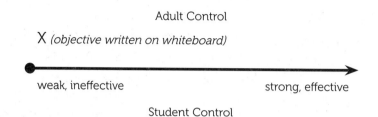

In an L2L context, we would contrast looking for the written objective in the classroom with determining whether students understood it well enough to explain it. Where might we place that student behavior on the continuum? Vertically, we're fully in the realm of student control, so that would indicate a placement below the line. In terms of effectiveness for learning, having students be able to articulate the objective is fairly high, locating it toward the right end of the line. Therefore, the continuum might look something like this:

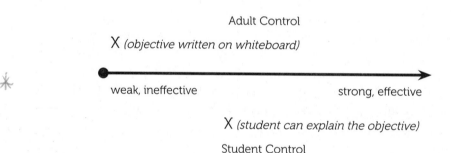

As you might imagine, this teaching-learning continuum is very useful in helping walkthrough observers understand that they should focus on behaviors that are "below the line." It also provides classroom teachers with a map for shifting the focus in their own classrooms. This shift in thinking (and the concomitant shifts in classroom practice) has the capacity to initiate powerful and fundamental schoolwide changes. Indeed, we have seen it replicated across the country. The following is but one example.

In 2008, a team of three site-level administrators from Boise, Idaho—Dr. Betty Olson, Liz Croy, and Dr. Kelly Cross—attended our first Engagement Conference. They wanted to know more about our work with student engagement and were especially interested in Look 2 Learning. They left the conference excited, seeing potential for L2L not only in their own schools but also for the entire district. They presented what they learned to a district leadership team, which quickly championed the program. Since then, L2L was implemented in every school in the district, became part of the district's strategic plan, and served as a common vocabulary for school improvement. Each school has a Look 2 Learning coordinator who assists the principal with data collection, scheduling, and reflection.

Dr. Olson, in particular, has used Look 2 Learning as the foundation for transforming her school. In 2010, she became principal at South Jr. High School and was determined to help the school become more learner-focused. The transformation has been transparent, incremental, and—frankly—amazing. Engagement and thinking levels have risen, lectures are rare, and discipline has improved. We recognize that Look 2 Learning didn't singlehandedly cause this change. The principal and staff still had much heavy lifting to do, but L2L provided a guide and monitoring tool for the school's evolution. It has become so much a part of the school's culture that if you sit down beside a student in class, he or she is likely to turn to you and whisper, "OK, here's what we're working on today…"

For us, talking to students has made all of the difference. Our walks (17,124 and counting) encapsulate more than a decade of insights gained from classroom visits. They have occurred in all kinds of schools: preschool through high school, urban and rural, large and small, needy and affluent. No matter where you work, the data presented in this book invariably include schools very much like yours and are gleaned from kids very much like yours. (We have found that, overall, there is a larger discrepancy between classrooms within a school than there is between schools. In fact, we have had to begin disaggregating data for schools and districts with which we work extensively.) Our conversations are usually informative, often insightful, sometimes funny, and occasionally moving. Here are a couple of them.

In early December, we walked into a 2nd grade classroom in South Carolina with the school's principal and assistant principal. A little boy looked up at Jim, made a terrible face, looked to the assistant principal, and then put his head down on his desk, sobbing. We all looked at one another and weren't quite sure what was going on. The assistant principal leaned down to whisper to the little guy, but the boy loudly said "I can't believe you really did it!" before putting his head back down. The assistant principal first looked puzzled but then started to laugh. She called us into the hall.

"That young man is one of my 'frequent flyers,'" she told us. "Yesterday, he was in my office for the third time this week. Out of frustration, I told him that if he didn't begin behaving himself, I was going to call Santa Claus. Well, Dr. Garver, when he saw you, I guess he thought I did!"

On another occasion, we were in a school somewhere west of the Mississippi. Again, it was close to the holiday season. In almost every classroom, we saw students engaged in a task with red and green construction paper. Finally, in one classroom, we saw something different: 2nd grade students coloring a calendar. The numbers stopped on the day in December that was the beginning of the school's holiday break. We tried to determine whether one of the students understood that she was working on a calendar activity.

"What do you think those numbers stand for?"

"They're just numbers. We have to count them."

"Do you do anything with this after you're done coloring?"

"We stick cotton balls on it and cover up the numbers."

"That sounds like fun."

"It *was* fun when we did it in kindergarten. In 2nd grade, not so much."

Several of the schools with whom we work are implementing Document-Based Questioning, a process that allows students to explore complex social studies questions by examining authentic historical documents. We recently visited a 4th grade classroom where students were really buzzing. Original sources had been distributed, and groups of four were considering the question "Why did so many people die at Jamestown?"

We stopped by one group to listen in on the conversation. The students were carefully poring over the documents when one of them spoke up.

"I think I have a reason." He had been looking at the ship's manifest—a list of the passengers and the cargo. "There aren't any women on this list. When women aren't around, men are like pigs. They don't even wash their hands. I think the men all got dirty, sick, and died."

Actually, that's a pretty powerful insight.

Those are a few of our experiences listening to the learners. What would your kids say?

Mrs. Garcia said in English that some people in class did not know what to write in their journals so today we were going to use them for thinking and we should just write for a minute and then we will do something together in them second block.

<u>My Reflection</u>: Today we did something cool. We played with candy. Mrs. Garcia gave everybody M+Ms and snickers and told us to make a venn diagram. Then we worked with a partner to tell how the candy was the same or different. She said we could only put one thing each in our venn diagram and then she was going to check them. I put that M+Ms were round. Then Patrick put that snickers were rectangles. Then she said Good job because those go together. She made us bring my journal up to put under the projector so everybody could see and we had to tell the class why they would go together. I didn't know why, but Patrick said cause they both had shapes.

She said Good job, so what if we move the word shape to the side since that's what we just compared. Then she said put something else about the candy. I put chocolate in the middle since they both had chocolate. Then she asked the other kids if the chocolate was the same in M+Ms and snickers. Every body said different stuff. Carla said the chocolate was on the inside in M+Ms and on the outside in snickers. Mrs. Garcia asked if we could move chocolate to the side since it was a BIG idea. After we did some more she told us all to keep working but to think about what each line was gonna be called. Patrick and me put television on one of our BIG lines and talked about the commercials.

M+Ms   snickers

shape   round   rectangle

brown?

chocolate   inside   chocolate outside

color   red blue   brown
    green yellow

tv adds   act like   make you be
    people   yourself

2

How to Use This Book

As we make the shift from teaching to learning, what could be more appropriate than looking at classroom life and work through the eyes of a student? Jerrod is a 7th grader who will share with us his thinking, learning, and growth as he experiences the school year. Rest assured, he will express his thoughts honestly, and we may even encounter a little rebellion and a developing sense of humor.

So, who is Jerrod? We'll tell you a few things about him and let you fill in the blanks. As we said, Jerrod is in 7th grade and is 12 years old at the beginning of the school year. He has one sibling, a sister named Jessica who is in 9th grade. Jessica does very well in school, but Jerrod thinks she is a bit of a drama queen. To the right, you will see Jerrod's 5th grade school picture (due to some inappropriate gestures, the principal will not release his pictures from the last two years).

Based on this information, and looking at him in the picture, what do you know or believe about Jerrod? (Take just a minute to think about it. Have you ever worked with a student like him?) When we asked teachers and principals this question, here are some of the responses we received:

- He is smart.
- He gets easily bored.
- You have to watch him like a hawk!
- If you can hook him and get him interested, no student will work harder.
- He has a wicked sense of humor.
- I would like to have a student like him in every class—but only one!

Jerrod has been very helpful for us. Early on, we used to talk in generic terms about "planning for kids." This is admirable, but it's almost a platitude. Planning for kids and their learning sounds nice, but planning for Jerrod's learning? That may be a bit more challenging.

Although shifting the focus from teaching to learning is a simple idea, it is not an easy one. When we were young teachers, we became adept at "shower planning." What does this mean? Step under the spray of hot water, lather up, and ask yourself, "So... what are we going to do today?"

With observations and evaluation systems that are based upon a teacher's presentation and performance, you can successfully plan while taking care of your morning routine. In other words, you can "shower plan" teaching, but we have learned—through experience and reflection—that you can't shower plan the facilitation of learning. The process is more demanding and complex than that.

We hope that this book will serve as a compass, a map, and even a means of transportation for this journey. A compass provides focus and makes sure you are moving in the right direction. We believe that, with reflection, these chapters will serve the same function. The book is a map in the sense that developing learning-focused plans to guide instruction is an essential part of the process. Finally, the strategies and tools presented can serve as a vehicle, moving classrooms toward deeper thinking, more engaging work, and higher levels of student achievement.

Across North America, schools are moving toward collaborative leadership models, particularly the establishment of professional learning communities. One of the considerations in the design of this book is that it should be appropriate for group discussion and book studies. Each chapter concentrates on a specific part of the planning process and can be used to drive, direct, and facilitate the shift toward learning-focused practice. Examples for classroom use and implementation provide the opportunity for testing new ideas and techniques. Group members can share and inspect their results, looking for patterns of success.

However, you do not need to be part of a professional learning community or engaged in a book study to gain insights and practical ideas from this book. An individual teacher interested in improving his or her practice will find opportunities for personal growth and reflection. Real-world stories and examples from schools and districts across the country encourage learning from the successes—and mistakes—of other educators. Though some may require a bit of adaptation or generalization, the tools and strategies found within can be implemented across the curriculum and with students of all ages.

To make the book as user-friendly as possible and to provide a consistent structure, certain elements will be included in every chapter. Each of these elements will be indicated by an icon to identify them clearly and reinforce each of their purposes.

Features of Each Chapter

Jerrod's Journal

At the start of each chapter, 7th grade student Jerrod shares some of his reflections on classroom experiences. His journal entries connect directly to the content of each chapter and help the reader see instruction through the eyes of the learner.

Look 2 Learning Data

A unique feature of this book is the inclusion of data from more than 17,000 classroom visits. These data provide a look at the current reality in classrooms across North America and offer a benchmark for evaluating individual classrooms, schools, and districts.

Research

Striving to base our work on the best and most current thinking in education, each chapter includes the research (including the researcher(s), findings, and implications) upon which the section is based.

Conflict and Consensus

You might not believe it, but occasionally the two of us have disagreements! In a point-counterpoint format, we'll share some examples of the real "cognitive dissonance" we've experienced and how we (usually) came to agreement.

Tools

We know that teachers appreciate practical strategies for immediate implementation. We've included some in each chapter, along with the opportunity to generalize them for adaptation across grade levels and content areas.

School Stories

Working with hundreds of schools across North America has allowed us to see what works—and what doesn't—in the implementation of a learning-based approach. Those stories are shared here.

To Think About

Occasionally, people with whom we work will say, "Wait a minute! I want to write that down!" Therefore, we have included a few thoughts meant to inspire your reflection.

Closure

We all know the importance of closure to learning, yet in our 17,000 classroom visits, it was rarely observed. Each chapter will end with a closure activity.

As we hope you can see, we have tried to make this book as practical and user-friendly as possible. Even though you will encounter many tools and strategies that are ready for classroom application, we will still ask for some reflection and transfer from you. When sharing our work in schools and districts, we are often asked to work with large groups of teachers who serve students from kindergarten through high school and teach across the content areas. We make a conscious attempt to include appropriate examples that span a wide variety of grade levels and content areas, but—invariably—a teacher will approach us after the session and say, for instance, "I'm disappointed. You only had one 3rd grade math example."

Likewise, in this book, we have made an effort to provide tools and strategies that reflect the spectrum of school subjects and grade levels. We ask that you take the time to generalize and transfer them for use in your practice. As you read each one, consider the following questions:

- What makes this work?
- Where does the shift from teaching to learning occur?
- How is student thinking raised?
- Why would students be more engaged?

Once you have identified these "big ideas," you can apply, modify, or even improve the tool or strategy as you incorporate it into your own designs for student learning. Here's an example of how this transfer might play out.

As mentioned in Chapter 1, we have discovered the power of using a continuum to organize, expand, and quantify thinking when learners (both students and adults) are asked to consider complex concepts. The graphic representation is an arrow that extends to the right, indicating an increasing level of intensity or impact.

We saw this tool used to great effect in a high school social studies classroom in upstate New York. Students were learning about women's roles throughout U.S. history, including their actions, achievements, and contributions. The teacher asked the class to list six women who were especially noteworthy. Here is the list they generated (in no particular order):

Susan B. Anthony	Pocahontas
Rosa Parks	Sandra Day O'Connor
Hillary Clinton	Amelia Earhart

Framing the continuum as a timeline, the teacher first asked the class to (quickly) place the women in a chronological sequence. He then divided students into groups of four and changed the focus of the continuum. The groups were asked to discuss the contributions of the six women and then place them on the line according to their impact on the lives of women in the 21st century—from "not at all" on the left to "crucial" on the right. As you might expect, the conversation was loud and passionate. After coming to consensus, students recorded their continua on chart paper and shared them with the class. None of the charts presented by the seven groups was identical to another, yet all were supported with solid reasoning and concrete examples. In the following class discussion, one young man said, "Looking at it this way, there may be other ladies who aren't as famous who should be on the list."

We often share this story, and it recently struck a chord with a kindergarten teacher from Arizona. Her students were learning about plants, and she decided to use the continuum approach to help them. Below is a copy of an e-mail we received from her and which is a perfect example of what we mean by *transfer*.

John and Jim,

After hearing you guys talk about using the continuum, I decided I wanted to try to use it with my little guys. It worked so well, I just had to tell you about it!

I first started, as you recommended, by figuring out why it worked, how it made the thinking better, and why kids were more engaged. I think it works because students have to express opinions and support them. I think the thinking is better because students have to look at one idea across multiple examples. I think they are more engaged because they get to have their own ideas and to talk to each other. There is also more than one right answer.

My kids have been learning about plants and what they need to grow and survive: water, soil, sunlight, and air. After a brief discussion, I turned them loose in groups. They were to use the continuum to show how important the four elements were to plant life. My surprises started quickly.

As one student in a group made an argument for water as most important, another said, "Unh uh, not for cactus! It's not very important at all. For them, water goes back at the beginning." (We do live in Arizona, after all!) The little group turned to me with puzzled faces and I knew I was having one of those monitor-and-adjust moments.

I said, "Wait a minute, boys and girls. Let's try this differently. Maybe different plants have different needs. Let's have this group do cactus, this one do grass, this one trees, this one flowers, and this one seaweed. Now let's try again." Not only were the discussions better—coming to consensus, sometimes rare for 6-year-olds—but they even added things. For instance, the flower group said, "We have to have bees. And they're important, too. Close to the arrow!" Of course, they loved sharing their work with the class, mostly because it was different and expressed *their* thoughts. The thinking and learning were amazing.

Before we move on, here is an activity that will provide closure for this chapter, allow you to experience the continuum as a learner, and serve as an anticipatory set for the rest of the book. Earlier, we mentioned that each chapter would have several common features, represented by the icons below.

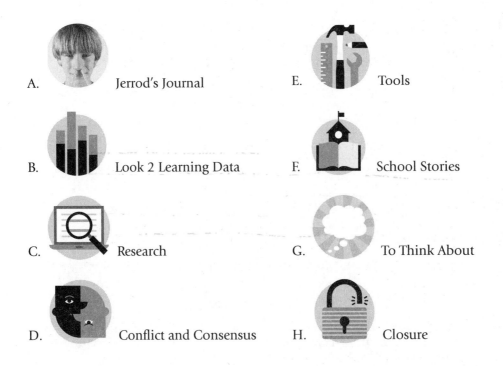

A.   Jerrod's Journal

B.   Look 2 Learning Data

C.   Research

D.   Conflict and Consensus

E.   Tools

F.   School Stories

G.   To Think About

H.   Closure

Place the letters for each icon on the continuum below. Use their relative positions to indicate which you believe will be the most effective or influential in helping to shape your thinking about the shift from teaching to learning.

Later, you can come back to see if your first impressions held true.

End of the Week Reflection:

Something I learned or enjoyed learning about

My favorite thing we did this week was the candy thing. We got to eat the candy when we finished but what I liked the most was how fun the venn diagram was. Instead of just filling it in we had to think whatever we thought. Mrs. Garcia was right when she said it wasn't about candy but about the lines. We did another one about the two stories we read this week and I learned that it didn't matter what you read as long as you could figure out the lines. We called the lines traits or attributes for the rest of the week.

I LIKE WAR!

Last night I was watching a tv show about the civil war and I started thinking about the big ideas in all of the battles and the wars. I think that winning is a big attribute but you only win if you have artillery, strategy, location, number of troops and stuff like that. These would be the lines.

I think Im good with traits!

3

Thinking and the Brain

Raising student thinking levels has been a teaching concern for decades; Bloom's taxonomy was first published in 1956 (Bloom, 1956). How to accomplish this feat has been the subject of much research and discussion. Some educators believe it's all about questioning. (It's not, as we will explain in this chapter.) Occasionally, we'll hear someone say, "You have to start low. Students can't get to higher levels of thinking until they've mastered the lower ones." To address that contention, let's visit two classrooms, seen in the same California district on the same day.

In the morning, we visited a middle school language arts classroom. The teacher was young, male, and enthusiastic—it was obvious that the kids liked and respected him. The students were struggling a little as we walked in, and the following was on the interactive whiteboard:

PERSONIFICATION:

the attribution of human traits, qualities, or actions to an inanimate object

- The dried leaves danced in the breeze.
- The chair complained as the heavy man sat down.
- The sun kissed the spring flowers.
- Oreo: milk's favorite cookie.
- My computer hates me!
- The dirty dishes cried for attention.

The students had been asked to generate more examples, and they were saying things such as "SpongeBob SquarePants" and "Mickey Mouse." Although one can understand their line of thinking, their examples were characters—more person than personification. The teacher began to explain the concept in another way as we left the classroom.

That afternoon, we visited a 4th grade class. It was Monday, so the students were becoming acquainted with their vocabulary words for the week. On the whiteboard were these three photographs:

The teacher said, "Boys and girls, look at the three photographs on the board. You'll see an elephant, a mountain, and a sequoia tree. See the man standing beside the tree? I want you to work with your elbow partner. One of you will need to be the recorder, and the other will be the reporter. You will have 30 seconds to find as many patterns as you can in the three pictures— things that are true about all three. OK? You have 30 seconds. Go!"

(If you would like to be a 4th grader for a few minutes, please participate. Find as many patterns in the photographs as you can. Go ahead; we'll wait for you.)

"Alright, our time is up. Let's hear how many different patterns we noticed. We'll start over here with Manny and go around the room. Check the pattern if you hear someone else say it, so we don't have duplication. Manny?"

"They are all big things; that's what we think," Manny replied.

"Let's test that, class," said the teacher. "Are they all big things?" The class agreed that they were. "Let's hear some other patterns."

"They are all things that people didn't make."

"You usually find them outside."

"They are all rough."

"They all have trunks."

"Let's talk about that," interjected the teacher. "Tell me about the second picture. Does the mountain have a trunk?"

"Well, there's green on the mountain. Those might be trees, and there would be trunks on them."

"Since we don't know for sure what the green is, we don't know for sure that they all have trunks. Do you have another pattern?"

"Could you climb all of them?"

The patterning continued until the lists were exhausted. Then the teacher said, "You found lots of patterns! Did everyone find the pattern of size—that they are all big?" (They all had.) "Then let's play with that idea. Same partners, switch roles. You have 30 seconds again. Think of all of the words you can that mean 'big.' Go."

(If you're participating, make your list now.)

After 30 seconds of animated conversation, students started offering their "big" words.

"Large."

"Huge."

"Gigantic."

"Massive."

"Enormous."

"Ginormous."

The class generated more than 20 synonyms before the teacher said, "I heard a word over here that I really liked: *massive*. Isn't that a cool word? That's going to be one of our vocabulary words—*massive*. I'm not going to give you a definition to memorize. You told *me* what it means. You gave me more than 20 synonyms! So, all you have to do is remember the connection you already made and the spelling: m-a-s-s-i-v-e."

And the class repeated this process for each of the 11 other vocabulary words. As you think about the two classrooms—"personification" and "massive"—consider the following questions:

- Where would you rather learn?
- Which method of instruction was likely to be more effective?
- In which classroom was the thinking level higher?
- What do these two anecdotes say about the need to begin at lower levels of thinking and build to higher ones?

Jim: So, the first content-rich chapter of our book is about thinking.

John: Yes, and I think it's totally appropriate that we begin there. But determining the beginning of the book was almost the end of our partnership. Do you remember that?

Jim: I sure do. We were working in my kitchen in Phoenix. We both understood the importance of the first meaty chapter since it really says where we think the teaching-learning shift should start.

John: I thought the book should begin with knowing your learners—our current Chapter 5. We are teaching kids after all. Don't we need to start there and look at the learning from their point of view?

Jim: That's important, but we aren't just playing with them all day. We have specific content to teach. That's why I thought we should begin with what is now Chapter 4: learning targets.

John: As I recall, it was a heated discussion.

Jim: I'll say! You had a hissy fit. You folded your arms and said, "If that's what you really believe, then I'm not sure I can be your partner anymore."

John: I'm not sure it was *that* dramatic.

Jim: It was pretty dramatic. But that's OK. It told me how strong your beliefs were.

John: And yet, here we are starting with a chapter on thinking and the brain.

Jim: After a lengthy and sometimes spirited discussion, we decided that's where the intersection is.

John: You can't get very far talking about students without considering how the kids will experience and process the content.

Jim: And likewise, content in isolation is of little use. It's only when kids internalize and apply it that it gains meaning.

John: After we decided to begin with cognition, it didn't really matter which chapter came next.

Jim: So, you'll still be my partner?

John: Stop it.

Attempting to develop an operational structure that describes the function of an organ as complex as the human brain is no easy task. One of the most comprehensive efforts was begun by Benjamin Bloom and his colleagues in 1948. They began by recognizing that the brain operates across three domains: cognitive, affective, and psychomotor. The cognitive domain is concerned with thinking and learning. The affective domain encompasses feelings and relationships, and the psychomotor domain deals with the brain's control of our physical movements. Though a taxonomy (i.e., an organizational pattern) was developed for the affective domain, it was the taxonomy for the cognitive domain that became the most relevant for educators (Bloom, 1956). The six levels of thinking were defined as the following:

- Knowledge
- Comprehension
- Application
- Analysis
- Synthesis
- Evaluation

Although Bloom's taxonomy became ubiquitous in undergraduate education coursework, a practical application didn't immediately find its way to most K–12 classrooms. We think part of the reason for this may be because it wasn't modeled for most preservice teachers. How was it most often taught and assessed? Unfortunately, it was at the lowest levels of thinking: "List the six levels of Bloom's taxonomy." If examples were requested, teachers had probably memorized those as well.

We review the work of Bloom and his colleagues frequently. For one thing, it is the oldest protocol with which we work. (Several versions of a so-called New Bloom have been published, but none seems to have taken hold definitively. Another system is set forth in Webb's Depth of Knowledge [Webb, 2005], but this framework was designed primarily for aligning testing with standards and not for planning instruction.) As you might imagine, we also do a lot of reading about the human brain and how it functions. Over and over, we see the word *patterns*—after all, the brain is a pattern-seeking device (Jensen, 2005). Indeed, we look for patterns in the world around us from the time we're babies (Medina, 2008).

Therefore, we decided to look at Bloom's taxonomy through the lens of patterns and brain research. Would it hold up? Would it still have relevance? Do the six levels continue to make sense? What we found was that they not only made sense but also gained new power and clarity when viewed this way.

Knowledge: The learner is given a pattern and then asked to repeat it (e.g., spelling tests, math facts, elements of the periodic table, historical dates).

Comprehension: The learner is given a pattern and then asked to paraphrase or extend that pattern (e.g., "Give me another example of personification").

Application: The learner is given a pattern and then finds a use for it in a new situation (e.g., students learn how to calculate the area of a rectangle and then use that knowledge to find the area of a triangle).

Analysis: The learner finds the pattern(s) by himself or herself (e.g., "Look at these three pictures and find as many patterns as you can").

Synthesis: The learner creates, combines, or ignores patterns (e.g., students are asked to find what makes the work of Vincent van Gogh and Georges Seurat unique and then create a painting that combines the styles of those two artists).

Evaluation: The learner is asked to compare patterns (e.g., "Read these two short stories, decide what makes a story scary, and then—using examples from both texts—write a five-paragraph essay that answers the question 'Which is scarier?'").

Based on these definitions, here is what we have seen in all of the classrooms we observed.

Levels of Bloom's Taxonomy	
Low *(knowledge, comprehension)*	87%
Middle *(application, analysis)*	9%
High *(synthesis, evaluation)*	4%

Look 2 Learning sample size: 17,124 classroom visits

Wow. Those are some startling numbers. We are often asked why we believe that middle and higher levels of thinking are so infrequently observed. We have several hypotheses.

- The percentages are about what we would expect to see in classrooms that are heavily teaching focused. In this environment, students are passively receiving information, which they later repeat, reproduce, or restate.
- If we focus professional development on better teacher questions or presentation styles, these data are unlikely to change. This is especially true if questioning strategies (raise hands, call on one) or assessment techniques (fill-in-the-blank, one correct answer) are not modified. (These data represent the thinking level of the tasks that all students are required to complete—not the responses of one or two volunteers.)

- Attempts to improve student engagement without concurrent efforts to raise the thinking levels of student work can lead to learners enthusiastically participating in low-level tasks.
- Many standardized assessments are perceived as testing at very low levels. In addition, many educators believe that the best way to prepare students for these low-level tasks is with rote instruction.
- We inadvertently condition students to perform at low levels by helping too much. When we then ask students to raise their level of thinking, we find that fear, old habits, and the need to be "right and done" stop them from successfully meeting the request. For an example, see the following anecdote.

In one partner school district, we were trying to build better writers from kindergarten through high school. One goal was to break free from an over-structured writing program that had elicited the identical papers with a templated beginning (My name is _____ and I'm going to tell you about…), middle (The first reason that… The second reason that… The third reason that…), and ending (Clearly, you can see that…). To shift away from this, we developed lessons that involved students dissecting anchor papers—exemplars of great thinking—and papers that lacked substance and style. As students scored and evaluated the model papers, they analyzed and identified the traits of an effective persuasive essay. In our original estimation, this was a great plan. While students analyzed the anchor papers, a number of teachers followed up by distributing a "helpful" framework of a so-called good paper.

Although we did have many valuable "aha" moments in classrooms, we were disappointed that some students simply substituted one recipe for another. For example, take a look at the following paper, which is taken verbatim from what the student actually handed in:

> I think we should not wear school uniforms state your opinion. Preview your first reason is that uniforms take away your personality. Preview your second reason is that it makes everybody robots. Preview your third reason is that some people have spent a lot of money on clothes they would not be able to wear. Wrap it up by restating your opinion that school uniforms are a bad idea.

> *In our 17,124 classroom walks, we saw middle-level thinking most frequently in kindergarten and special education classrooms. The lowest overall levels of thinking were recorded in high school advanced placement courses. Why might this be so?*

Another question we are frequently asked regarding our Look 2 Learning data is what the percentages for thinking levels *should* be. It is a question we do not answer directly. Ideally, the data would reflect the distribution of thinking levels across the state standards, state testing blueprints (if available), and intentional efforts to provide scaffolding within complex concepts and skills.

We do believe this: The key to raising thinking in a meaningful way is to focus on the middle two levels of Bloom's taxonomy, application and analysis.

Application

The human brain likes to gather useful information and then find ways to employ it. In the real world (and in the world of Bloom as viewed through the lens of patterns), there is an implied separation in time between the learning of a new tool or strategy and the use of it. This is the challenge of performance tasks on some of the newer, more rigorous state assessments.

Traditionally, we provide students with new skills and frameworks, practice them, test them, and then move on to the next concept. In assessment systems that are more authentic, skills, strategies, formulas, ideas, and information are learned and then stored in a student's "mental toolbox." When a challenge is presented—at some later date—the student examines the problem and then sorts through his or her toolbox to find an appropriate tool that can address the problem. Being comfortable with this separation between learning and application will set the stage for raising thinking levels in general.

Analysis

Finding patterns is one of the most natural ways for our brains to learn. Far too often we see curricula, programs, and lessons in which patterns have been found for students and then given to them for digestion and regurgitation. If we revisit the "personification" and "massive" stories from the beginning of this chapter, we might find a pattern there. The teacher in the middle school language arts class structured his lesson in a very logical order, the way teachers are taught to do.

1. "Here is a new term we're going to learn about."
2. "This is what it means."
3. "Here are some examples."

Once students had sufficient background knowledge (as in low-level thinking), they were able to talk about this new idea. By contrast, the 4th grade teacher altered this order. She recognized that very few of the concepts we teach are totally foreign to our students—even though the terms for them sometimes might be. Here is what she did with the order of her vocabulary lesson:

1. "Here are some examples."
2. "You find the big idea."
3. "Oh, by the way, here is the term for it."

Notice that the students began with analysis (pattern finding) and then moved to knowledge (receiving the word and its spelling). There is a catch-phrase that we like to use for this shift in order: *Zip it and Flip it!* In other words, say less and change the order—let students explore and structure concepts before providing more conventional, standardized content. (Please note that the word *flip* is not being used here as it is often used in some other educational circles. There, it means providing video lectures for students to watch at home and then using class time for practice, questions, and checking for understanding. We simply mean changing the order in which students interact with content.)

There is another reason that we suggest beginning with efforts to encourage more middle-level thinking. True synthesis and evaluation cannot occur without analysis. Learners cannot create, combine, ignore, or compare patterns unless they have first identified them. In fact, once analysis has occurred in the classroom, we often see students moving to higher levels of thinking on their own—creative types move to synthesis and critical thinkers gravitate toward evaluation.

In countless classrooms, we have seen students who are all over the Bloom spectrum. One student is performing analysis while another works at the knowledge level—on the exact same task. We recognize that students think differently, but a learning task should be designed to guarantee a predetermined minimal level of thinking. Again, it's not the questions teachers ask or the manner in which they present content that matters; what's important is the thinking level required by the work.

Let's return to the comparison task that Jerrod described at the beginning of Chapter 2: filling out a Venn diagram for different candies. In this task, Jerrod and his classmates are allowed to enter the information pertaining to each candy at the knowledge level. However, his teacher very quickly directs the task and student thinking to the application level. By focusing the conversation on the lines, she guides learners to find, define, and ultimately refine the patterns in their thinking.

Let's experience this as the learner. Below is a traditional Venn diagram that purports to compare Arizona and Arkansas, the home states of the authors of this book.

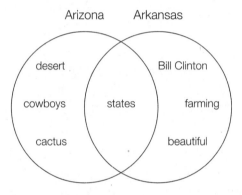

Though the answers are all appropriate, they do not demonstrate a thinking level required of the comparative task—analysis or application. We invite you now to participate in an activity using an adaptation of the Venn diagram that will move the thinking level of this task toward the middle. Let's start again, with only one idea placed in the graphic organizer.

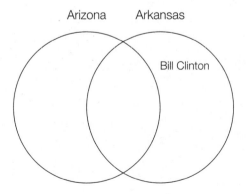

Now we force a thinking shift. We will add a line beneath the name Bill Clinton and extend it through the Venn diagram. Your task is to decide what the "name" of this line is. In other words, what is *Bill Clinton* to *Arkansas*? How are they related? Before you read on, we encourage you to write down a possible line attribute or category.

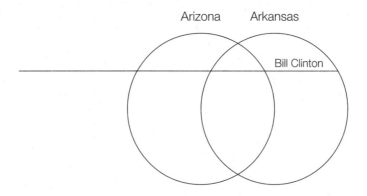

Experience and background knowledge will certainly come into play as students analyze the relationship between Clinton and Arkansas, providing quite a range of possible answers. If we want to call the line *presidents*, then there is no parallel answer for Arizona. (Sorry, Jim.) If we change it to *presidential candidates*, then the Arizona equivalent might be John McCain or Barry Goldwater. Calling the line *famous people* would still allow Barry Goldwater to be correct, but it also allows for other possibilities, such as Stevie Nicks or Emma Stone. For the sake of continuity, let's move forward with *presidential candidates*. Note that there is nothing in the overlap section—"similarities"—for this category. It might be silly to try to find a similarity. The goal of the Venn with Lines diagram is to challenge and enhance thinking, not to fully complete a graphic organizer.

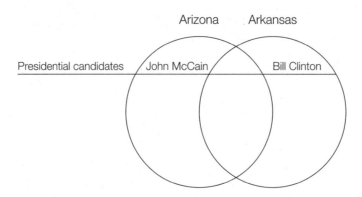

Certainly, Arizona and Arkansas are both beautiful states, but rather than simply moving the Arkansas descriptor *beautiful* to the middle of the Venn diagram as a similarity, we'll place it outside the graphic and propose it as a category. When we sat and discussed what made Arizona uniquely beautiful, Jim placed *desert* back into the Arizona circle. John decided the word *green* best described his state's natural beauty when contrasted with Arizona.

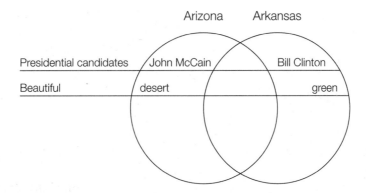

Can you find a similarity in the *beauty* of Arizona and Arkansas? If so, please place it in the middle of the diagram.

To fully model the shift in thinking, the following Venn diagram is "completed." See if you can find how all of the ideas from the original (lesser) diagram were revised, combined, or coerced. Can you follow the thinking?

Arizona   Arkansas

	Arizona		Arkansas
Presidential candidates	John McCain		Bill Clinton
Beautiful	desert		green
Pioneer figure	cowboy		Spanish and French traders
Agriculture	lettuce citrus	cotton beef	soybeans
Native plants	cactus	pine	hardwoods

As we ourselves completed this task, the inclusion of *cowboy* was a bit of a contentious issue. John understood the category of *pioneer figure* but was unable to name a different figure for Arkansas. It would have been easy to move *cowboy* to the middle (after all, his former school district did produce three state rodeo queens), but he wanted more out of the activity. This impasse called for a bit of research. That's when John learned that the original pioneers of what was then called Arkansas Post were French and Spanish fur traders.

We have seen this phenomenon repeated in classrooms in which the thinking is pushed to the middle. Students who are working through their own content patterns—yet do not have all of the answers—will voluntarily go and seek more information. As a student, if my teacher asks me a question, then I'll give him or her the answer if I know it. If not, I'll shrug it off. However, if I ask myself a question, then I'm more likely to seek out an answer that satisfies my own curiosity.

Why is this true? In short, because our brains are wired this way. In 2008, molecular biologist John Medina published his book *Brain Rules*. The title refers to 12 big ideas (or rules) about what science knows for certain about how the brain works. We would love to give a classroom example of each and every rule (and certainly could), but the parameters of this book do not allow such a luxury. Instead, we've presented and summarized each rule with a possible implication or connection to education.

Exercise

Rule #1: Exercise boosts brain power.

Our ancient ancestors were constantly moving and working. They never sat still for 50 minutes, let alone 6.5 instructional hours. Exercise provides the chemicals necessary for better cognition: more blood is pumped to the brain, bringing glucose and oxygen. Movement stimulates the protein that keeps neurons connecting.

Simply running on the playground for 30 minutes can make a major difference in the mind's ability to concentrate. Recess and PE are not interruptions to the day; they are a boost to cognition.

Survival

Rule #2: The human brain evolved, too.

Human beings possess a triune brain. In other words, we have three brains that comprise the whole brain. The first is the reptilian brain that is all about survival and physical safety. The second brain is the mammalian brain, which is concerned with relationships within the "herd." Finally, the cortex is the cognitive brain where thinking and learning occur. All three brains must be working in concert for cognition to happen. (Although this structure was originally designed as a theory of the vertebrate brain, it still serves as an apt metaphor for the changing focus of the brain—driven by elements in the environment.)

Wiring

Rule #3: Every brain is wired differently.

Regardless of class size, no two students will process or store information in the same way (or even in the same parts of the brain). Even though a teacher might provide the exact same auditory and visual instruction to all members of the class, each student hears and sees the information through his or her own unique lens of experiences, emotions, and connections. The learning is not the same, even if the activity is. Therefore, it is important that learners be allowed to articulate to someone—not necessarily the teacher—how their minds are connecting to the new content.

Many kindergarten teachers have experienced this when students hear a story about a cat and then feel a sudden need to share stories about their cat; a neighbor's cat; Grandma's cat; or how Grandma went to Disneyland (without her cat), rode a roller coaster, and got sick.

Attention

Rule #4: People don't pay attention to boring things.

The brain pays attention to that which captures or arouses our emotions. Something that makes no connection to me is boring. However, if we are going to talk about me and my world, then I'm in.

Activities that allow students to identify a central idea or explain the patterns they see help the brain accept key details introduced later. The gist of the content becomes glue for the parts.

Short-term memory

Rule #5: Repeat to remember.

As learners, we process information by encoding and storing it—sending it to different regions of the cortex for storage. A student who draws a picture representing elements of the academic content will end up storing diagonal lines from the drawing in one part of the cortex, while vertical and horizontal lines are stored in two additional locations. If we add color to the picture, we incorporate additional storage. The more storage "spots," the more likely we can retrieve the information when we need it. The more elaborately we encode a memory during its initial moments, the stronger its retention will be.

Although music, movement, and visuals definitely enhance memory, introductory activities that force learners to find patterns within new content make even the recall of information more consistent and long-lasting. In other words, the sooner kids move to the middle, the better.

Long-term memory

Rule #6: Remember to repeat.

While many of us were trained as teachers to have students repeat ideas many times during a lesson, we may have missed the most important component of repetition. Perhaps a weight-training metaphor will explain this best. Nobody gets stronger by lifting heavy dumbbells 100 times in a row; we actually may traumatize our muscles and do damage. At best, our muscles will tire quickly and give up. Physical trainers know that the number of repetitions is not as important as the number of sets performed during a training session.

Back in the classroom, drilling math facts for 30 minutes is not nearly as powerful as 10 minutes of multiplication at 9:00 and another 10 minutes of practice before going to lunch. Finally, at 2:30, we have a final 10 minutes of math facts. The intervals of rest and practice do more for the brain than a longer sustained stretch.

Sleep

Rule #7: Sleep well, think well.

Because the brain replays what we have learned during the day—and continues to rewire itself during the night—sleep may be as important to achievement as the classroom activities themselves. Loss of sleep negatively impacts attention, executive function, working memory, mood, quantitative skills, logical reasoning, and motor dexterity.

People vary in how much sleep they need and when they prefer to get it, but the biological drive for an afternoon nap is universal. Since it is unlikely that nap time will be built back into our schedules after preschool, we might find activities or moments that allow the brain to experience the trancelike state of sleep. Activities that involve mundane, noncognitive, psychomotor movement (e.g., walking a treadmill, playing in a sandbox, manipulating sewing cards, or cutting out shapes) allow the brain to take necessary "rewiring" breaks.

Stress

Rule #8: Stressed brains do not learn the same way as non-stressed brains.

When we humans experience emotional stress, we produce cortisol, a chemical designed to work with adrenaline to get us away from the stress—whether that is something or someone who could physically harm us or make us feel humiliated, wrong, or wronged. The worst kind of stress comes from situations over which we feel no control. Laughter, movement, and food can counter these feelings of helplessness and cause the body to slow or reverse the production of stress chemicals; they can even trigger the production of serotonin and dopamine—chemicals necessary for cognition.

Teachers sometimes protect their most stressed students from tasks that require high levels of thinking. We call this the "bless their hearts" mentality. Ironically, the exact opposite would be more beneficial to a chronically stressed learner. Providing a student with an emotionally safe activity that requires him or her to identify patterns, argue, and defend his or her thinking may actually provide a sense of cognitive control and a break from stress outside the classroom.

Sensory integration

Rule #9: Stimulate more of the senses at the same time.

In order to make the encoding of information more elaborate, and therefore more powerful, learning activities should be designed to stimulate multiple senses at the same time. Rather than simply reading a speech by Eleanor Roosevelt, high school students who watch a video of her delivering the speech and then reread the speech later end up with three different cognitive pathways for storing the information. Two pathways—sight and sound—occurred simultaneously, whereas reading the written word accounts for the third. This approach also incorporates the idea of interval training from Rule #6.

Vision

Rule #10: Vision trumps all other senses.

Half of the brain's resources are dedicated to the sense of sight. It is interesting how much of our early years are spent connecting what we see to sounds and other senses. For example, the softer, prettier parent is called Mommy. She smells of vanilla. The one with the moustache and lower voice is called Daddy.

If the learner is unable to recognize, or "see," the concept in the curriculum, can we reasonably expect him or her to learn it? Activities must be designed to incorporate visuals or to conjure them up in each brain.

Gender

Rule #11: Male and female brains are different.

Although there are differences in the structural and biochemical components of male and female brains, there is no difference in cognitive ability or capacity related to gender. In the classroom, work that incorporates emotional connections increases the likelihood that girls will remember details and boys will get the gist.

Exploration

Rule #12: We are powerful and natural explorers.

From birth, humans begin testing their surroundings through observations, hypotheses, experimentation, and conclusions. We look for patterns and try them out. It is an active, rather than passive, process, and we take control of and interact with our environment. It is the most natural way we learn.

On John's fifth day as a new kindergarten teacher, his students taught him the lesson of Rule #12. Three boys were in a far corner of the playground intently staring at something on the ground.

"Hey boys, what are you doing?"

Michael called me over. "Look at this bug, Mr. A."

Davis added, "Watch this" before he leaned over and screamed at the beetle.

The bug continued on its straight path.

Michael and Jeremy each took turns screaming at the bug. The beetle continued forward.

Davis provided a summary: "Bugs can't hear! But watch this." He then raised his right leg as high as he could and brought it crashing down into the grass just in front of the beetle. The beetle promptly changed direction.

Michael stomped, and the beetle turned again. Then Jeremy took his turn, and the beetle changed course a third time.

Davis summed it all up: "Bugs can't hear, but they can *feel*!"

This was an ideal opportunity to teach. "That's because insects have these special extensions on their heads called antennae. They use them to…"

As John rambled, the boys ran away. They had already captured the learning. They did not want to stick around for the slide presentation and lecture. Alas, antennae will have to wait for another day.

Like Davis and his friends on the playground, now it's your turn to make sense. For closure, consider all that we've seen in this chapter about thinking and the brain. Formulate a claim or compose an arguable opinion about learning and thinking that can be supported by what you've read. What evidence would you use from the text to support your claim? Can you imagine how someone might question or disagree with your claim? Record your responses below.

My claim:

_____

_____

Evidence from the text to support my claim:

1. _____

2. _____

3. _____

What is a counterclaim to my position?

_____

_____

WORKING WITH YOUR TABLEMATES,
WRITE SIX QUESTIONS YOU HAVE
ABOUT TODAY'S OBJECTIVE:

ANALYZE HOW A POEM'S FORM
OR STRUCTURE CONTRIBUTES
TO ITS MEANING.

1. Are we going to have to write poems?

2. Why is it always about flowers and lovey kissy stuff?

3. Are there any poems about war?

4. Is rap poetry?

5. Could we do this with a song instead?

6. Why do you have to know about poetry?

4

Learning Targets

Standards, essential questions, objectives, outcomes, and targets—these are the names given to what we teach our students. It is—as we argued in Chapter 3—an obvious place to start the teaching-learning cycle. After all, how do we begin instructional planning without knowing what our learners should be able to?

When you take a family vacation, don't you typically know where you want to go? Is the goal of the trip to see the Grand Canyon or to camp along the outer rim? Or is it to laugh and sing along the way in the car? Is it important to stop for gas? Should you plan the return trip, or just wait and see how it goes? Oh, and did anybody feed the cat before you left?

On the other hand, you might just decide to head west. This sort of adventure might appeal to some, whereas others would be completely paralyzed without travel guides, notebooks, packing lists, and a GPS. It could also result in a wide range of possibilities, including a life-changing experience or a new place to call home.

"Heading west" in the classroom may allow for great adventures, but it seldom guarantees the outcomes specified in the standards.

Recently, a North Carolina school district asked us to conduct a "Snapshot of Learning," during which we visit multiple classrooms on the same day, collect data about learning, and then look to the data for trends and patterns. In the morning, we visited elementary schools and saw 3rd grade students learning about fractions. The children were working in groups of three, and the teacher had given each group an envelope containing nine cards. The first card had the word *right*, the second card had the word *acute*, and the third card had the word *obtuse*. The other six cards depicted various angles. The teacher asked students to organize the cards in some way that made sense. (Since this was the beginning of the lesson, dictionaries were available if students required them.) Much discussion ensued as various frameworks were proposed for how to arrange the cards.

In the afternoon, we visited secondary schools and saw 8th grade math students concluding a unit on geometry. Students were creating posters—using glitter, neon markers, and puffy paint—to represent right, acute, and obtuse angles.

Even though the standards for 3rd and 8th graders might have intended for students to learn about angles, it is doubtful that these tasks were aligned with the appropriate levels of rigor described. The 3rd grade students were engaged in analysis (finding patterns), but the 8th grade students—although excited about the glitter—were operating at the knowledge level (repeating patterns).

In our classroom visits, we see a lot of teaching "about" various topics with a clear lack of specificity regarding the criteria for demonstrating appropriate levels of learning.

Topic Alignment *(with activity scaffolding toward the verb)*	78%

Look 2 Learning sample size: 17,124 classroom visits

Our figure regarding topic alignment is a simple, single number, yet it represents a variety of ideas. The 78 percent figure refers to the amount of time that students are involved in an activity about the standard. The remaining 22 percent includes other classroom activities, such as taking attendance, cleaning up after lab experiments, lining up, and teaching content not specifically related to the standards.

A word of caution is necessary here. This figure masks the relatively low frequency at which learners are actively performing the standard independently and as written. Although scaffolding activities are necessary to break a standard into smaller, more manageable learning targets and skill sets, they are only a part of the learning journey that culminates in the larger, more complete academic performance as required by the standard.

Let's explore a musical metaphor. The Chicago Symphony Orchestra performs Mahler's Fifth Symphony on three consecutive nights of concerts. We will call this the performance of the standard. A week prior to the first performance, the orchestra holds a dress rehearsal. In three earlier rehearsals, the conductor worked on particular passages and excerpts with the musicians in order to elicit his interpretation of the piece and provide practice in the difficult transitions.

For a month prior to the performance, the musicians each spend hours practicing their individual parts of the symphony. However, as any musician knows, an inordinate amount of time is spent practicing: scales, long tones, arpeggios, and exercises of tone and technique. Without the practice and repetition of these basic skills, the musicians would be unable to apply them to the much more complicated piece of music. Nevertheless, mastery of these skills alone does not guarantee a successful performance.

Likewise, as teachers, we must recognize that simply teaching *about* a standard will not deliver the results we want to see in our students.

One framework to help create intentional, focused lessons is described in *Understanding by Design* by Grant Wiggins and Jay McTighe (2005). Often referred to as backward design, the process has teachers set clear, measureable targets before they create instructional activities. The stages of backward design can be seen in Figure 4.1.

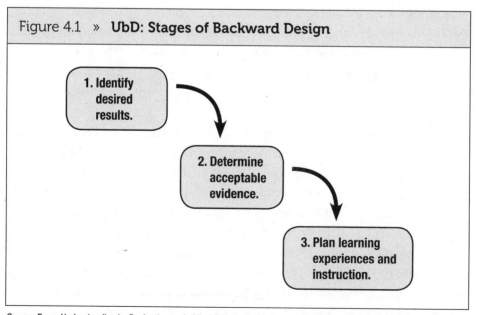

Figure 4.1   »   **UbD: Stages of Backward Design**

1. Identify desired results.

2. Determine acceptable evidence.

3. Plan learning experiences and instruction.

Source: From *Understanding by Design* (expanded 2nd Ed.), by G. Wiggins and J. McTighe, 2005, Alexandria, VA: ASCD (p. 18). Copyright 2005 by ASCD.

Identify desired results: What should students know, understand, and be able to do? These outcomes typically come from standards, curriculum expectations, and pacing guides.

Determine acceptable evidence: How will we know if students have achieved the desired results and met the standards? This can include both formal and informal evidence of student understanding and proficiency.

Plan learning experiences and instruction: What activities will equip students with the necessary knowledge and skills? By choosing activities and strategies after clear, measureable results have been identified, instruction becomes more purposeful and intentional.

Important decisions must be made in each of these areas, but much of the real work of instructional design lies between the boxes in Figure 4.1—in the arrows. How do we translate the results we desire into behaviors we can measure? And how do we create tasks and experiences that lead to these measureable outcomes?

From Results to Evidence

Before we examine the importance of determining acceptable evidence for desired results, let us first say that we are great believers in the power of the "non-example." Looking at what goes wrong can often provide illumination and guidance for moving forward more effectively.

An extension of the Look 2 Learning classroom walkthrough process allows teachers and their leaders to "walk" a lesson plan. Often used in PLCs, this tool defines research-based structures and look-fors that allow participants to analyze, reflect upon, and refine instructional design. Although the process requires a high degree of trust within the group, the objective nature of the instrument helps to create emotional safety and prompt constructive conversations. The backward design elements are among those for which we inspect.

Recently, a group of Illinois teachers met to discuss plans for upcoming units. One of the teachers brought with her a lesson from a free online lesson design website. The activity looked interesting, so one of the teachers suggested that they inspect it for design qualities. The rationale and sequence seemed to be planned well, and the activity looked like fun. However, when they examined it from the perspective of backward design, they were shocked. The lesson purported to teach geometric shapes by having students create a design for a home, yet on a 10-point assessment rubric, only one point was allocated for geometry and math. The other nine assessed neatness, materials used (extra points for glitter!), and a subjective judgment of how "interesting" the design was. If the rubric were shared with students before they began the project, mathematical learning certainly would not have been the explicit target.

From Evidence to Activities

Let's look further into the idea that the effectiveness of a task may be impacted by who is in control of it. In order to experience this from a learner's perspective, we ask you to participate and complete the following tasks rather than simply read them as examples. (We recognize that the choice to participate is yours, but we encourage you to jump into this process of "shift.")

TASK A

Parameters:

   With a watch or timer available, allow three minutes to complete as much of the task as you can. Your answers must be handwritten on a piece of paper. You may use any technology or resource available, but the grade/score will only come from what you write onto a piece of paper.

Task: All the States

   List all 50 U.S. states in alphabetical order, and identify the capital of each one.

Now that the three minutes are up and the task has ended (even if it wasn't completed), count the number of states you correctly recorded in alphabetical order for a subtotal of up to 50 points. To that number, add the number of correct state capitals you recorded. How did you do? A perfect 100 percent? A passing score? Congratulations on your participation.

   Now, let's move onto to a second task.

TASK B

Parameters:

   This is a collegial task. Since you may be reading this book on your own, we have included a way for you to be part of a small collaborative learning team. Complete the first part of the task in writing and then, in the second part, compare your answers with those of the authors.

Task: Moving to a New State

Imagine you are being forced to leave your current state of residence. You must relocate to a different state. Before you can decide on where you want to live, you must list three criteria (considerations or attributes, not actual states) that are important to you and your family as you look for a new home. Then, for each of these criteria, identify a simple question whose answer will help you narrow your list of choices.

For example, suppose that John had identified the ability to have a garden as one of his criteria. His questions might therefore be: *Which states have distinct seasons?* or *Which states grow the largest tomatoes?*
Record your criteria and questions in the following space:

Criteria   Search Question

1.

2.

3.

Now that you have recorded your thoughts, we want you to talk with your imaginary friends John and Jim and share, compare, and combine your thinking.

John

Criteria	Search Question
1. gardening	Which states have distinct seasons?
	Which states grow the largest tomatoes?
2. airport access	Which airports have the most direct flights to U.S. destinations?
3. music	Which cities have symphony orchestras and major concert venues?

Jim

Criteria	Search Question
1. no snow	Which states have the least amount of snowfall?
2. big city	Which cities offer arts, theater, and major sporting events?
3. politics	Which states are known to be politically moderate or conservative?

Your task now is to come up with some large categories, concepts, or social studies constructs that capture these collaborative ideas. For example, *climate* might incorporate John's desire to garden and Jim's dislike of snowfall. Alternatively, *hobbies* might allow John's gardening to be combined with Jim's theater outings. Please find at least three such "groupings."

1. _____

2. _____

3. _____

Reflection

Now that you have completed Tasks A and B, we have a few reflective questions for you.

1. *Which task did you enjoy more? Why?*

Many people prefer Task B because it gives them an opportunity to think about themselves and make a personal response with no wrong answers. They often share that Task B also gives them a chance to get to know their collaborators and learn more about them. At the same time, people with a competitive nature sometimes prefer Task A—which involves racing against the clock. Others prefer this task since technology more or less guarantees a correct response, and the task provides the security of right and wrong answers.

In other words, some people find Task A "engaging," whereas others prefer the engagement of Task B. In Chapter 6, we will discuss the meaning of *engagement* and the engaging qualities of student work a bit further.

2. *Which task did you find to be more difficult? Why?*

Some people find Task A to be difficult, especially if they try to complete it from memory, without any resources. Others find Task A quite easy since they can still recite the "state rap" they learned in elementary school—"Fifty Nifty United States." Others find Task B to be more difficult because it requires some thinking, whereas Task A relies on rote memorization or just copying from a website.

Even though we may not agree on the difficulty of the two tasks, we should be able to agree on the cognitive demand of each task. Using the language we introduced in Chapter 3, we can consider Task A to be a low-level task. If you had the states memorized, the task was one of simple recall. Even if you actually alphabetized the states as you recalled them, it still remains a task of low cognition. If you copied the state list from a website or book, then there was absolutely no cognition required once you began to copy.

By contrast, Task B—choosing and finding categories for the criteria—involves the middle level of Bloom's taxonomy. Finding and naming the patterns of *climate, recreation, politics, safety, economics,* or *demographics* moves the cognition to analysis. If you found that John's entry for gardening could fit in *climate* but was actually better placed in *economics* (since he plans to sell his tomatoes to earn some extra cash), then you and the rest of your collaborative team were working at the evaluation level.

Let's be clear: level of difficulty and cognitive demand are not interchangeable. What is easy for one student may be difficult for another, yet analysis is still analysis.

3. *Which task is a standard?*

In the 38 states in which we have worked, no state has a social studies expectation for students to list all fifty states alphabetically. However, many states do expect students to locate states by region or read maps to identify the names of major cities, geographic features, and the relative sizes of states. Task A might ring true as a task many of us did in school, but it is not a standard in a 21st century curriculum.

By contrast, Task B may not *sound* like a standard—indeed, it is not; it is a task of learning. It does, however, take us directly to a standard that exists in many states at both the elementary and secondary level: Students will be able to identify the reasons people move or immigrate from their ancestral homes, communities, and countries. A generic list of examples typically follows this standard, including political, economic, cultural reasons. Task B almost always generates appropriate categories, thereby satisfying the standard.

> *It's hard to hit a target you can't see.*

In our original, teacher-focused walkthrough model, we asked, "Has the objective been clearly communicated to the learners?" As we shifted the focus to the other side of the desk, that question became inappropriate. The data we collect now measure whether the learners can clearly articulate the objective. To accomplish that effectively, students must first *personalize* it. ✳

In Florida, we had the opportunity to work with the staff of a small private school. The school is so small that the principal is also a part-time teacher. Our work included visiting classrooms with the principal, analyzing and discussing what we saw. During one of these sessions, the principal said, "Let's stop by my classroom first." So we did.

It was a 6th grade language arts class, and students had just finished reading an allegorical story. One of the symbolic characters was a dragon. We spoke to a boy in the front row.

"What are you working on today?"

"Drawing a picture of a dragon."

"Wow, that looks cool. What do you think that's supposed to help you learn about?"

"Probably just to help us remember what's in the story."

"Are there certain things you're supposed to include in your picture?"

"Nope, just draw a character... and mine's the dragon."

As the young man went back to his drawing and we stepped out of the classroom, the teacher/principal was dumbfounded.

"I don't believe it," she said. "I wanted to go to my classroom first because I *just* gave them the assignment! We've been studying allegories, and this last one is very typical. They were supposed to choose a character and include elements that depicted what that character represents in the story. I gave them an example from the story we read on Tuesday. Their picture was supposed to have at least three clues to show what the individual or creature symbolizes. That boy is not shy; he's one of my most articulate. I explained it, but because it didn't mean anything to him, he couldn't."

In our experience, when students have personalized the objective, they can verbalize it clearly—in a variety of ways. The data below represent a baseline, gathered from schools where helping students personalize the objective was not an explicit part of professional development.

	Baseline
Students can articulate what they are doing.	93%
Students can articulate what they are learning.	33%
Students can articulate why they are learning.	9%
Students can articulate what success looks like.	4%

Look 2 Learning sample size: 12,237 classroom visits

As you can see, the percentages decrease as we move down. This occurs because the questions we ask to determine these data are in a progression of sophistication and depth of student understanding. The numbers also decrease because of their inclusive relationship. In other words, the classrooms in which students can articulate what they are learning (33%) are a subset of the first category (93%).

In an elementary school in Virginia, we were training teacher leaders in the first phase of the L2L process of data collection—articulation of an objective. Each "walking team" consisted of a trainer and four teacher leaders from the school. As part of the training exercise, the five team members would enter a classroom, and each of them would select a student to interview about the objective. After leaving the classroom, they shared what their selected students had said and discussed the learning task. We spent all morning visiting classes from each grade level and had some very powerful experiences and conversations.

One of the trends we noticed was that during reading activities, students struggled to articulate what they were learning, even though they could definitely articulate what they were *doing*: "We're reading our books about dinosaurs." When asked what they were learning to do, however, they often repeated the content of the story: "We're learning about dinosaurs."

At the close of our morning session, one of the participating teachers shared her disappointment that the majority of the intermediate students with whom we spoke were unable to identify the appropriate learning objectives. She mused aloud, "I wonder what *my* 5th graders would have said."

"Let's go find out."

"No! It wouldn't be fair. Since I'm part of this training, there's a substitute in my room!"

"Barbara, if we were looking at *teaching* today, it might not be fair to walk into your classroom. However, we're looking at *learning* today. With or without you present, your students are at school today, and you probably planned for them to work in your absence, right? We can certainly look at their work and their learning."

As the five of us entered the classroom and spread out through the students, I could see the look of concern on Barbara's face. The students were all silently reading Chapter 14 of *Old Yeller*, but they graciously stopped to answer our questions.

When we met outside in the hallway to compare notes, we discovered that our five selected students gave the same answer to our first question about what they were doing: "We're reading Chapter 14 of *Old Yeller*."

We then shared the student responses to our second question about learning.

"We are learning about a boy and his dog."

"We're learning about context clues."

"It's a good book for boys."

"Vocabulary."

"We're learning that a dead bull stinks."

While we all chuckled at the last response, Barbara began to get emotional. "That was not good. I'm so upset that they can't tell me what they are learning."

"But they just did. Are you unhappy about what they said?"

"Yes."

"What would you have hoped they would say?"

"Well, I chose that novel because some of my boys don't like to read and it captures their attention. We were working on context clues and vocabulary yesterday. Of course I want them to read for comprehension."

"I think that's what the kids just told us."

Barbara was not satisfied with that answer, and the visit to her classroom was weighing heavily on her heart.

The next week, a new group of L2L trainees walked through the school, including Barbara's 5th grade classroom.

When we asked kids in the three 5th grade classrooms what they were learning, every single student showed us a laminated bookmark, which is shown in Figure 4.2.

"Well, I'm choosing to make a prediction about what will happen next in the story and telling why I think that."

"We are learning to read and make connections. This part about Lisbeth makes me think about how my little sister is a pest, but I still love her."

"We're doing a bookmark activity anytime it makes sense or by the end of the chapter so we'll be better readers."

Those of us who made visits on both days—a week apart—saw a dramatic difference in the students' articulation of learning. They moved beyond simply repeating what they were doing to explaining what they were learning. They described a combination of skills and the relevance of reading a book about a boy and his dog.

Figure 4.2 » **Reading Bookmark for Self-Monitoring**

Writing as we READ
Choose one of the following to write about in your reading journal during or after reading.

Predict
What do you think will happen next in the book? What evidence do you have for this?

Infer
What inference can you make about a character in the story? What evidence from the text supports your inference?

Evaluate
What judgments can you make about a character in the story? What evidence from the text supports your inference?

Making Connections
Text to Self
What in the text reminds me of my own personal experiences?

Text to World
What in the text reminds me of the world around me? (movies, TV, news)

Text to Text
What in the text reminds me of another story I've read?

In Chapter 1, we used a continuum to represent effectiveness (left to right) and the release of control from teacher to student (top to bottom). Writing an objective on the board and hearing a student explain that objective were plotted on the continuum, and the results looked something like this:

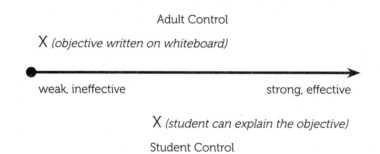

The teaching-learning shift is represented by classroom practices that tend to move down and to the right. For practice, where would you place the following on the continuum?

- The teacher and students read the objective together.
- The objective is printed at the bottom of handouts and tests.
- Using standards, students help write the objective.
- We see students using the bookmark shown in Figure 4.2.

Of all of the look-fors in the L2L protocol, *students articulating the objective* is perhaps the easiest one to move. Yes, it begins with a teacher behavior, but if the teacher chooses carefully, the learning behavior changes very quickly. A few years ago, we were asked to work with a school in South Carolina that had just been assigned a new (but experienced) principal. The teachers at this school had been working hard to implement several initiatives, but they seemed to lack clarity and vision. After visiting each classroom with the new principal, we met to discuss the data.

"It seems to me," he said, "like a great place to begin would be with the objective. I don't see how our kids can move very far until they know where they're going." Students' understanding of what they were learning and why it was important became the focal point around which school improvement efforts were organized.

Because the data for this component move quickly, we have disaggregated them for our partner schools (such as this South Carolina school) where personalizing the objective has been made a priority. Here, the baseline percentages are compared to those from our partner schools.

	Baseline	Partners
Students can articulate what they are doing.	93%	93%
Students can articulate what they are learning.	33%	67%
Students can articulate why they are learning.	9%	42%
Students can articulate what success looks like.	4%	18%

Look 2 Learning sample size: 12,237   4,887

When teachers communicate learning expectations clearly and consistently, students not only notice but also appreciate it. During a visit to a school in Idaho, a teacher shared with us a drawing that was created by one of her students. It was submitted in a life skills class, and the assignment had been to share a message about good nutrition. The self-portrait submitted by Jordan Alcorn (shown in Figure 4.3) certainly conveys this message effectively, but notice the whiteboard in the background. We had worked with teachers in that district to help students personalize *what* they would be learning, *why* it was important, and *how* they would experience the content. These elements had become so much a part of classroom expectations that this student, quite naturally, included them in her drawing.

John: Relevance is certainly a powerful connector in instruction, isn't it?

Jim: It's one of the most powerful; our brains crave it.

John: Yet, why do we see it used so infrequently in most of the classrooms we visit?

Jim: I think it's that sometimes we, the adults, can't always figure out why kids need to learn some of the content we have to teach. We hear this a lot from secondary teachers of higher-level math. When was the last time you used an imaginary number?

John: I have always struggled a little bit with most of the second languages we teach. I understand the relevance of Spanish. In many areas of the country, it would be very helpful to know. But why are we teaching German?

Jim: Do you think it's because of tradition?

Figure 4.3 » **Healthy Habits: Articulation of Learning Targets**

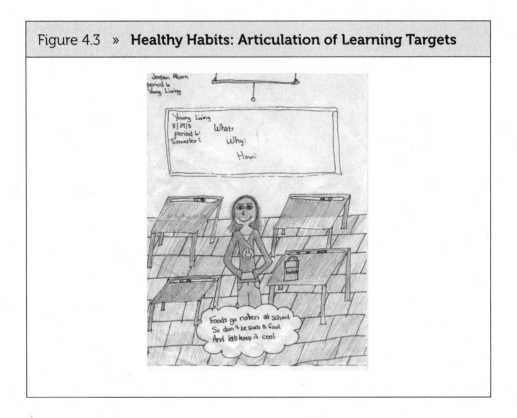

John: Sometimes it's necessity. At my high school, we offered French because Madame Williamson was willing to move back to Arkansas after living in Paris.

Jim: So, let's take these two areas—higher-level math and second languages. Can we find any relevance there?

John: Well, I was lucky in that Madame Williamson was a great teacher. She helped us understand that, by studying French, we were really learning more about the constructs and features of our own language.

Jim: No matter what the language, there is some degree of authenticity. Real people speak it somewhere in the world.

John: Or in the case of Latin, *spoke* it.

Jim: Touché.

John: Back to the relevance of French.

Jim: I always thought there was something about the sound of another language that was fun, too. French poetry has to sound different in French than an English translation read in English.

John: *Oui.*

Jim: On to the higher-level math.

John: This can be hard, because math teachers love math! There is almost an assumed passion for it and appreciation of the beauty of its structure.

Jim: Which many 14-year-olds may not recognize.

John: I do think we can help students understand that there is a unique way of thinking within most disciplines—a mathematical way of thinking, a scientific way of thinking, a social science way of thinking...

Jim: And many careers require those entering to be fluent in those languages, too.

John: *C'est exact.*

Jim: Enough already with the French. I think that in addition to relevance, there's another *R* word that could be of use here: *Relationship.*

John: I'm not sure what you mean.

Jim: If we take the time to talk about relevance when it's appropriate, kids will trust us. Then, when something isn't especially applicable, we can explain that and the kids will be more likely to come along with us.

John: *Certainement.*

Jim: Is that it?

John: *Au revoir.*

Jim: Madame Williamson would be very proud.

We invite you to compose your own task of closure for this chapter. From the columns below, select a voice, a product, and an audience in order to explain or illustrate an important idea from this chapter.

In the voice of...	Produce...	For an audience of...	Purpose
A 5-year-old	A drawing	Angry villagers	
A fly on the wall	A commercial	People who disagree with you	
A sportscaster	A sticky note	A school-board member	To explain or illustrate an important idea from this chapter
A parent of a troubled student	New lyrics to a familiar song	A talk-show host	
The president of the United States	A map	Aliens from another planet	

November 5

Awesome! Today in English, Mrs. Garcia said we were
going to begin working on our argument writing and
research project and that we could pick from a
list of topics to argue in our history class. She said
that one of the hardest parts of this assignment
would be to recognize other claims and establish
ours as more reasonable.

One of the topics on her IDEAS page was that
the Battle of Gettysburg was the Turning Point
of the Civil War. Are you kidding me! Most people
think that's true, BUT I know the TRUTH and the
class needs to know it too.

**Mrs. G., when you put this on the list, did you
know this would be the one I would pick?

The Battle of VICKSBURG was the turning point
because that's when the Union took control of

the Mississippi River—Probably the most important
weapon in the war.

I know that only 19,000 soldiers died during the
siege of Vicksburg and Gettysburg was like 50,000
but the river was the most important thing and
when the Union controlled it, they
> cut off Texas
> stopped attacks from the west
> and could trade with the world

Even Lincoln said Vicksburg was the key and that
the union could not win until the "key is in our
pocket."

I can't wait to start on this!

5

Know Your Learners

Jim: If I remember correctly, this chapter is where you wanted to start the book.

John: Yes, it is.

Jim: Help me understand that again.

John: As we learned in Medina's *Brain Rules*, humans—including our students—are egocentric creatures. We want to share our ideas and learn more about what is important to us.

Jim: And if, as instructors, we understand what is important to the learners, then we have a better chance of connecting our content to them, their interests, and their ways of approaching learning.

John: I think there's another reason I wanted to start with this chapter. If the big idea is shifting our focus from teaching to learning, then we have to consider kids and their environment when making this transformation.

Jim: For instance, you might teach earth science differently—making different connections, providing different examples—in an urban classroom than you would in a rural one.

John: As you know, my daughter is an interior designer. She can't start any design work until she meets with her clients and understands their tastes and preferences.

Jim: I like that word: *clients*. As professionals, educators have clients—our students—and we should get to know their needs, worldviews, and learning methods.

John: But I don't think that can be imposed on teachers until they understand and appreciate the need for it.

Jim: Wow, I'll say! When I was teaching high school, a teacher advisory program was implemented. Teachers were assigned 20 students, based on
an alphabetical list, to get to know and mentor.

John: I'll bet the teachers hated it.

Jim: Everybody hated it! Twenty minutes every day. Occasionally, we were
provided with lessons to conduct on study skills or life skills. It all
seemed like such a waste of time.

John: Why?

Jim: There was no reason to be there. None of us—teachers or students—saw
the point.

John: Oh, you egocentric humans!

Jim: So, I'm hearing three distinct and different ways that we should get to
know our learners. First, we need to understand what kids, in general,
"look like." How might they be similar to or different from how we were
as students? As people, what do they need and want?

John: Second, we should determine what *our* kids look like. Are there things
about our students' experiences that might affect their approaches to
school, learning, and content?

Jim: And finally, we need to consider what specific kids, such as Jerrod (or
Keniesha or Kwan or Camila) look like.

John: Sounds like a great organizational structure for the rest of the chapter!

There are no specific L2L data for this chapter. If we looked at how well
a teacher knows his or her students, individually or as a group, we would be
looking at an adult behavior—the teaching, not the learning. Having said that,
talking to students about their work and their learning, as we do in L2L visits,
is a wonderful way to get to know kids and how they think.

What Kids Look Like

Most of us probably remember studying Maslow's hierarchy of needs as undergraduate students (1993). If you were like us, it didn't mean a whole lot at the
time. There was no immediate opportunity for practical application. Like much
of the content of those education theory courses, we memorized the relevant
information, repeated it on the test, and then promptly forgot it.

As we begin to deal with real kids who live in a real (and sometimes not
so pretty) world, Maslow's ideas tend to gain newfound significance. As shown
in Figure 5.1, there are a variety of human needs that must be satisfied before

students are ready to deal with academic content in a serious way. Note that three of the eight needs—Safety, Belongingness, and Esteem—deal with relationships in the classroom and that all of them are prerequisites to cognition.

Figure 5.1 » **Hierarchy of Needs**

Hierarchy of Needs
(Basic to More Highly Developed)

Biological and Physiological
air, food, drink, shelter, warmth, sleep

Safety
protection, security, order, rules, limits, stability

Belongingness and Love
family, affection, relationships, work group

Esteem
achievement, status, responsibility, reputation

Cognitive
knowledge, meaning, self-awareness

Aesthetic
beauty, balance, form, creativity

Self-Actualization
personal growth, self-fulfillment

Transcendence
helping others to self-actualize

When we ask veteran teachers if kids have changed over the span of their careers, we usually get a quick reaction from one of the extremes—either "Not really, they still want to be loved and to know that they are a part of something" or "Absolutely! They're texting all the time and never without their devices." As we sit and talk through the question, though, they usually come to a consensus: kids are the same; the world has changed.

Central to that change is the role of technology. Although it is ever-present, we intentionally do not look for "technology" in the L2L protocol. Rather, we look at the work students perform while using technology. In many districts, we see a drive toward increasing the use of technology, but it is not always implemented in ways that benefit learners in their understanding of content, self-development, or interaction with the "real world." ☀

On the other hand, we have also seen that technology can increase autonomy, mastery, and purpose—the three most important predictors of high-quality work (Pink, 2011). For example, in classrooms where students develop and post online tutorials to help their struggling peers understand a concept, Maslow's cognition and transcendence come into play and the repetition of "another problem" now has purpose. In short, technology allows students to create, share, and contribute their ideas and products to the class, school, and world. However, without relationships, well-designed work, connection, and ☀ relevance, the mere inclusion of technology does not advance learning.

Perhaps an anecdote here will help to illustrate our point further. (This story has been around for years. An early version was told by Canadian storyteller Ron Evans.)

Electricity had finally come to the village! As the workmen arrived to run the power lines, the villagers gathered around the storyteller in the large open space that served as the community's social center and meeting place. They were all seated on the ground. As always, the people were listening with rapt attention, but the noise and activity of the work crew was too much. One by one, the villagers quietly stood and went to watch. Lines were strung overhead as the villagers stared, mouths open with amazement.

After everyone had gone, the storyteller retreated to the edge of the village circle, watching quietly and thoughtfully. Soon, workmen brought a stool and put it in the storyteller's usual place in the circle. On top of it was a television. They fiddled with the controls, and a picture jumped to life. The children came first, hearing the strange sounds and fascinated by the colorful pictures. Adults followed. Before long, the entire village was once again gathered in the clearing, except now they were watching the television. The storyteller still stood to the side, calm and silent.

A power company supervisor stopped by the village several weeks later to ensure that everything was working correctly. When he stepped into the village circle, he was astonished. The villagers were gathered on the ground and listening to the storyteller. The television had been moved to the side, still on its stool. The supervisor leaned down and whispered to a young boy, "Is the television broken?"

The boy whispered back, without taking his eyes off the storyteller, "No, it works fine."

"Then why aren't you watching it? The television knows many more stories than your storyteller."

The boy thought for a moment, and then looked the man in the eye. "The television knows many stories... but the storyteller knows me."

> *Technology is just a tool. In terms of getting the kids working together and motivating them, the teacher is most important.* —Bill Gates

What *Our* Kids Look Like

We often assume that our students, as part of the American "macroculture," share a fairly similar set of experiences, perspectives, and values. Though there are certainly common elements, differences within and among microcultures can provide significant variations that challenge schools and educators.

Ruby Payne (2013) uses economic class as a framework for understanding and describing differences in how people relate to society, institutions, and one another. She delineates three groups of people—those living in poverty, the middle class, and the wealthy—and then describes their "hidden rules" for living. For example, it's possible to look at how each group views and values time. For those facing poverty, the emphasis is on the present. Decisions are generally short term and based upon emotions or basic survival. Within the middle class, the future is most important; planning and deferred gratification are valued. Among the wealthy, the past is key. History and tradition are major considerations in their decision-making processes. Recognizing these differences might help us understand our students' attitudes toward deadlines and priorities.

Of course, there are other frameworks and factors that might help us understand the similarities and differences among our students. On the following pages, we present four stories that portray varying degrees of success by educators attempting to identify and address this diversity.

I. Culture

Several years ago, Jim had the opportunity to serve as assistant superintendent for curriculum and instruction in an Indiana school district. In that position, he oversaw the administration of state testing. The state had introduced a new test, and Jim was glancing through the items. One question asked, "Which of these do we no longer use?" Shown were four line drawings: a car, a plane, a horse and buggy, and a train." Jim thought to himself, "My daughter Amanda will miss this one—and so will all the other kids."

The school district was located in northeast Indiana—Amish country. The "correct" answer was that we no longer use horses and buggies, but the students in that school—"our students"—saw them every day. On the other hand, the train tracks in that area were being torn up to create hiking trails and bicycle paths. As educators, we know our students. Sadly, the testing company did not.

II. Experience

We recently worked in a school district with a significant refugee population. The topic was engagement. We were facilitating a discussion on authenticity—helping students see the connection between curriculum content and the world. One frustrated teacher said, "Do you know anything about our community? We get kids in our classrooms with *no* experiences."

We talked about that for a little while. These kids didn't just crawl out of an egg. They have experiences, just not *our* experiences. In some ways, their lives may have been richer and more varied than the lives of their (non-refugee) classmates. The implications are twofold. If we want to make our content more relevant, then we may have to learn more about students' backgrounds. In addition, if students don't have experiences upon which we can (or want to) build, then we may have to provide them.

III. Vocabulary

In a school district in a southern state, the state testing data turned out to be a great place to learn more about the children. The school and the state used a consistent test blueprint from year to year. As we looked at particular questions that proved to be troublesome for students, we noticed something interesting in the phrasing of some multiple-choice questions.

- In the story above, what makes the character Agnes unique in her group of friends?
- What is unique to the third list of numbers?
- What unique feature did scientists discover about the planet Uranus?

Do you see the pattern? It wasn't a reading or math issue. The students—"our students"—did not understand the word *unique*. The following year, 4th grade students throughout the district began the year writing about what made their summer experiences unique. Science, social studies, and language arts classes incorporated unique events and characteristics. Music and PE teachers also helped stress unique qualities and features during their time with students. After a year of "uniquing" in the classroom, we saw significant growth on the relevant state exam questions.

IV. Interactions

In another of our partner districts, a rural elementary school had just completed its comparative analysis of the district benchmark and state proficiency exams. For the fifth year in a row, there was a dramatic achievement gap between African American males and the rest of the students. We began to dig into—and discount—potential root causes. Poverty *could* play a role, yet other children in similar circumstances scored significantly higher. The fact that males among other demographic groups were performing better also debunked a gender-based explanation. Although it remained unsaid, we began to wonder if the teachers treated these students differently in the classroom.

The scores were not going to illuminate a potentially contentious issue such as this. Therefore, we decided to use the Look 2 Learning framework to further explore the situation. As we visited the first classroom, we interviewed an African American male seated with three other tablemates.

"Hey, what are you all doing today?"

The young man began to explain, "Well, first we have to read this passage..."

As he paused, one of his white classmates took over the explanation: "It's about recycling."

A young woman of color then added, "And we then have to find evidence that supports why we should do it as well as evidence why people might not want to do it."

This short moment might not be informative in and of itself, but we found a consistent—and troubling—pattern during our visits to fifteen other classrooms. Regardless of the grade level, content, or task, when our young black males initiated a conversation or answered a direct question, other students answered for them or even "took over" the conversation.

The L2L observations brought forth a question we would need to address as a faculty: Do these young men get the same chance to communicate and explain their thinking in the classroom?

Other questions we might ask about our students include the following:

- Do our ESL students have an opportunity to think deeply about content, given the additional time needed to process language?
- Are our students in remediation included in enrichment activities?
- Do our students have the support (and the resources) at home to complete independent projects?
- Is diversity among our student population hindering or enriching learning opportunities?
- How do school expectations for our students match what they hear at home?
- Do our special education students have access to grade-level standards in spite of lower reading levels?

What Jerrod Looks Like

As we have seen through Jerrod's journal entries, if we intentionally have students generate work, products, and responses that reveal their cognition, opinions, and attitudes, then it becomes much easier to get to know each of them. This knowledge, in turn, can help us design more effective and meaningful instruction.

In one California school district, the middle and high schools had chosen to focus their instructional improvement on the use of "bell-ringer" activities. The district provided teachers with a day of training during the summer about the new policy and shared various methods of how to incorporate the new strategy. The training was clear on the primary purpose of these bell-ringers—they were responsible for engaging learners and activating their prior knowledge.

As the school year approached, teachers were expected to use the first 5–8 minutes of class to "grab" the learners' attention, activate their prior learning, or elicit individual written responses to the question of the hour. The training discouraged using bell-ringers as a simple review or practice more than once a week. Rather, thought-provoking questions, prompts, or problems were to be provided for student consideration and response.

As teachers worked together to plan these bell-ringer activities, they made certain that the questions drew students to the objectives and standards they planned to teach. The collaborative nature of the planning also had the added impact of guaranteeing a cohesive implementation across course sections.

Throughout the semester, teachers met by grade level, department, and course to share student work and present evidence of implementation. During these short meetings, teachers analyzed student responses, refined their questions and activities, and continued to "grow" the practice.

As the second quarter began, we were invited to "audit" the secondary schools. Specifically, the district wanted to see if outsiders could qualify or quantify the perception that the bell-ringers were adding value to student learning. We used the Look 2 Learning protocols to collect information from more than 150 classrooms.

In our first three classroom visits of the day, we saw a variety of activities. In the first room—a language arts class—students were writing their reactions to an excerpt from the beginning of Dickens's *A Tale of Two Cities*:

> It was the best of times, it was the worst of times, it was the age of wisdom, it was the age of foolishness, it was the epoch of belief, it was the epoch of incredulity, it was the season of Light, it was the season of Darkness, it was the spring of hope, it was the winter of despair, we had everything before us, we had nothing before us...

Students were asked to write what they thought Dickens wanted the reader to think or feel at the beginning of the story—before the storyline or characters were even introduced. Students were also required to explain how they had experienced something similar in their own lives. Those who could not (or chose not to) respond personally were allowed to use similar storylines from television, movies, or other books for support.

The second classroom was a social studies class in which students were asked to draw a picture that represented the meaning of *manifest destiny*. Many students began to capture images of westward expansion and maps, whereas others drew abstract symbols such as dollar signs, crosses, and bags of gold. One student, who had drawn a simple arrow, was the first to explain her drawing to the class: "I don't remember ever hearing the words *manifest* and *destiny* together, but I drew an arrow to show that it is somebody's destiny to go from where they are to the future?"

A rise in the student's inflection let us all know that she was not sure of her answer, but she still felt safe enough to share it with the class. Two other students shared explanations with a bit more understanding of the content. As we exited the classroom, the teacher asked the other students to partner up and compare what they had heard in the three responses with their own drawings. This activity served to build a collective idea about manifest destiny among students.

In the third classroom, math students were working valiantly in small groups of two or three to try to solve a word problem written on the board:

> The admission price to a large flea market is $4.00 for adults and $1.50 for every accompanying child. If the admission booth collected a total of $6,495.50 for the day and the counter on the turnstiles registered 2,562 people, then how many children and adults entered the flea market?

In all three classrooms, students were highly engaged and were working at middle or high levels of Bloom's taxonomy. At the end of the day, the trend data proved to be very interesting. When we dissected the collected data, we found that the classrooms with the highest level of student cognition were those classrooms we visited during the first 10 minutes of class. In other words, the bell-ringer activities were paying off; student thinking and engagement had increased.

As a part of the audit process, teachers met to reflect on their implementation and practice. Many teachers reported increased engagement among their students. The consensus of the faculty was that the level of thinking, sharing, and academic dialogue was better than ever. More significant to this chapter, most teachers observed that the nature of the activities involving an individual written response that was followed by a short whole-class discussion allowed them to learn about their students and develop relationships with them much faster than was possible in the past.

Thirty years ago, Howard Gardner proposed that intelligence was not a single general ability but a series of modalities that served as entry points to understanding. According to Gardner, "we each have eight or more intelligences, and we can use them to carry out all kinds of tasks" (Gardner, 2006, p. 26).

The intelligences cover a wide range of abilities that humans incorporate to make sense of information:

- Musical
- Bodily-Kinesthetic
- Logical-Mathematical
- Linguistic
- Spatial
- Interpersonal
- Intrapersonal
- Naturalist

When we plan lessons for a specific group of learners, we want to start with the intelligences that are most natural and common for them. Building on this moment of comfort, we then want to include other intelligences in the work so students are stretched and the content becomes more connected.

We often talk of "planning from the other side of the desk," which means looking at content and activities from the students' point of view. Now imagine that a principal asks her teachers to do that, and one young teacher is struggling. As he sits in his classroom, he thinks, "What will kids think of this? How do I connect it to them? To *my* kids?"

The answers are elusive. As his mind wanders, his eyes land on a can of craft sticks he uses to call on his students. He reaches in and pulls one out. "Cassandra. How would I plan this lesson for Cassandra?" Suddenly, the planning has more purpose and more focus. Although this lesson might be tailored to Cassandra, the teacher knows that it will be productive and enjoyable for most of his kids. And tomorrow might be Juan's lesson. And the next day will be for Jasmine. Hey, this could be fun!

 The tool for this chapter is your own can of craft sticks—or gradebook or computer roster. Use it to select one student and then design a lesson for him or her. We believe you will help your students make more connections, be more engaged, and arrive at deeper levels of understanding if you approach planning with this mind-set.

What Kids See in You

By now, it should be very obvious how important we think the teacher-learner relationship is. We did, after all, dedicate this entire chapter to it. We have also discovered from our classroom visits that this relationship is built in both directions. In other words, it's also important for our learners to know who *we* are.

In a school district in Georgia, we were conducting an L2L visit in a 12th grade English class. After discussing the day's task, we asked the seniors about the classroom décor, which featured numerous posters of vintage aircraft and aerial photographs of wildfires. The students told us that the posters were not connected in any way to their readings of *Beowulf* or Brontë but were about Mr. Hansen, their teacher.

We were told that "Mr. Hansen has his pilot's license and is a trained smokejumper. Last year, he got called away for a couple days to help in the Yosemite fire. It's cool that he can do all that kind of stuff and still loves *Pride and Prejudice*."

In a classroom centered on reading, interpreting, writing, and the art of communication, it appears that personal relationships were still important.

There is an epilogue to this story. Three months later, we ran into Mr. Hansen at a regional luncheon honoring him and the other state teachers of the year. He shared with us how the school year had progressed and that his district had hired a different consultant to conduct walkthroughs to focus learning. In the feedback session, Mr. Hansen was instructed to remove the posters and photographs since they "did not connect to the lesson" that day.

Happily, Mr. Hansen's pictures remain on the wall.

Find the School Stories icon in this chapter, and select one of the four stories that you consider most powerful. For that story, complete the following closure activity:

Restate: Write a single sentence that captures the main idea.

_____

_____

React: Write your emotional reaction to the story.

_____

_____

_____

Remember: Write about a time in your own life as a leaner that is connected somehow to the story.

_____

_____

_____

Respond with Questions: Write three questions that are triggered by the story.

1. _____

2. _____

3. _____

Science was so cool today! (Mrs. Garcia, you would like it too.) We were given a big piece of paper that was supposed to be geologic record. Our group had to look at it to see if we could figure out what was going on. Everybody had to make a guess first on our clipboards and "cite evidence." (You'd like that part!) After everybody made a hypothesis, we then shared. Mr. Lee said if we all guessed the same thing, we would have to work together to find other possible ideas. We all said pretty much the same thing—it looked like one animal finds a little animal to eat and then gets into a fight with a third animal over the food. You could tell that the big animal from the southeast was just walking until he saw the other one with food in his mouth and then he ran to steal it (the footprints get farther apart as he runs). Then they stomp all over the ground as they are fighting for the food. (Their footprints are all mashed together.)

The funniest part was when Mr. Lee asked us to come up with another explanation using another animal behavior we studied.

Anna—who never talks—said she thought the one in the middle was a female and the one on the right was a male who chased her and then they mated. Michael asked about the little animal and Anna said "maybe he just watched?"

6

Engagement

Overall Engagement Level	
Engaged	6%
On-task	91%
Off-task	3%

Look 2 Learning sample size: 17,124 classroom visits

When educators first see these numbers, they are almost universally horrified—and often a bit defensive. One reason is that, as teachers and former teachers, we have a tendency to put percentages on a school grading scale, which doesn't recognize that a 90-80-70-60 standard of success might not fit every data set. For instance, the best batters in professional baseball might have a batting average of around .350. That means they only hit the ball 350 times in 1,000 times at bat. That equates to 35 percent—a low *F*—on a traditional grading scale. Nevertheless, that's still enough to make the player famous and earn him millions of dollars per year.

Another disconnect might be that we are operating with different definitions of the word *engaged*. How has our thinking about engagement evolved?

Up until about a decade ago, the word *engagement* was used in a binary way to describe student behavior—students either were working or they were not (although using the word *engaged* might have implied that students were following directions with enthusiasm). Then, in 2002, Phillip Schlechty published his seminal book *Working on the Work (WOW)*. In it, he describes not two but five different levels of engagement or, as he puts it, ways that students respond to work. His five levels are

- Authentic Engagement: The learner finds meaning and value in the work.
- Ritual Engagement: The learner completes the work to gain positive outcomes.
- Passive Compliance: The learner completes the work to avoid negative outcomes.
- Retreatism: The learner is not completing the assigned work but is not disrupting others.
- Rebellion: The learner refuses to do the work and actively disrupts the learning process.

During our Look 2 Learning classroom visits, we discovered that we could recognize different levels of student engagement, but discerning why students were on-task in a four-minute walkthrough was very difficult—and probably not especially significant. Capturing the fact that students are off-task can provide important data, but what they are doing while off-task is a topic for a book on classroom management, not this one.

Engagement happens (or it doesn't) for each individual student, but for the purposes of our L2L classroom visits, we recorded the engagement level of the entire classroom. In order to provide meaningful and succinct information, we collapsed Schlechty's five levels of engagement to three. A classroom visitor will generally witness one of the following scenarios:

- The Engaged Classroom: Most students are engaged in the learning, and all students are engaged in some aspect of the task. Off-task behavior is rare or nonexistent.
- The On-Task Classroom: The classroom is orderly, and most students are completing assignments willingly.
- The Off-Task Classroom: A significant number of students (generally 3–5 or more than 15 percent) are not participating or completing assigned tasks. There may be a fair number of students on-task, but engagement is rare.

This emphasis on engagement at the classroom level is an important one. Increasing student engagement does not have to be a districtwide initiative—or even a schoolwide one. Consider the well-known quote commonly attributed to Margaret Mead: "Never doubt that a small group of thoughtful, committed citizens can change the world; indeed, it's the only thing that ever has."

The following story illustrates this point beautifully as the vision of one became the passion of a few and led to changes in the practice of many.

Collins Hill High School (CHHS) is located in the greater Atlanta area and serves more than 3,000 students. In 2010, Kim Nichols, assistant principal of the school, attended a conference about increasing student engagement (presented and hosted by the authors of this book). Even though she already recognized that increasing engagement would enhance learning for students at CHHS, she left the conference with tools to share and a framework for implementation at her school.

To build a strong foundation for the work, Kim formed the CHHS Instructional Leaders Academy. This group of teachers volunteered to experiment in their classrooms with the engagement ideas Kim presented. The following year, in an effort to build leadership capacity, Kim invited key member of this team to join her as she returned to the Engagement Conference. Science teachers Donna Alswede and Laura Herbig, along with advanced placement social studies teacher Jon Aldrich, became the local experts and champions for this work at CHHS.

Three years later, their influence had spread across the school and positively influenced dozens of teachers and thousands of students.

> *Engagement for its own sake is just "fun." To enhance learning, students must be engaged in a cognitive verb.*

We occasionally hear from secondary teachers who don't understand the importance of the cognitive verb and explain to us how engaged students are in their lectures. The problem is that, more often than not, the students aren't *doing* anything. You can't be engaged in someone else's work; you can only be entertained by it. In fact, the thinking level of student work plays a critical role in the level of engagement.

The following table presents the interesting relationships—both causal and correlative—between thinking level and engagement.

Cross Tabulation Between Engagement Level and Thinking Level				
		Level of Engagement		
Thinking Level	# of visits	Off-Task	On-Task	Engaged
Low	14,898	4%	94%	2%
Middle	1,541	< 1%	71%	29%
High	685	0%	58%	42%

Look 2 Learning sample size: 17,124 classroom visits

As an example of how to read the chart above, when the thinking level was low (as it was in 14,898 visits), we saw off-task behavior in 4 percent of the classrooms, on-task behavior in 94 percent of the classrooms, and engagement in only 2 percent of classrooms. Note that when thinking shifts from a low to a middle level, students are 14 times more likely to be engaged (from 2 percent to 29 percent).

As a caution, we must remember that the numbers captured in the last column of the previous chart represent only the engaged-level classrooms (a total of 6 percent) of the original 17,124 observations. When we consider these 1,027 visits, we can look at the distribution of thinking in a different way.

Thinking Levels in Engaging Student Work	
Low	28%
Middle	44%
High	28%

Look 2 Learning sample subset: 1,027 of the 17,124 classroom visits

While this may look good for low-level thinking—that it leads to engagement more than we might have thought—keep in mind that the *vast* majority of our visits found thinking at low levels. The rate of engagement when thinking was at the knowledge or comprehension levels was still fairly negligible (i.e., 2 percent).

So, aside from raising thinking level, how else might we design work so it leads to more engagement? The answer begins, once more, with Schlechty

(2002). He describes 12 "standards" that would be present in a school or classroom that has engagement as a central tenet of its culture. We recognized that several of his standards deal with beliefs, conditions, and prerequisites, wheras others spoke more directly to the qualities of student work. In addition, Schlechty clearly states that his work is not research. Rather, he says that it is "a system of thought and a way of life" (p. xvi).

Therefore, we decided that—because we were actually *in* classrooms—we could do the research. After isolating eight qualities that could be included and observed in student work, we visited classrooms, looking at students' engagement levels and the qualities present in their work. We did that 5,000 times.

Some interesting things became apparent. Some of the qualities correlated with student engagement, yet some did not. We were as likely to see them in on-task classrooms as we were in engaged ones. Still others of the WOW standards needed to be adapted, renamed, or redefined to describe what we saw. For instance, one standard is Product Focus, yet we discovered that when the products that students were producing were identical, we rarely observed engagement. When they were unique and different—expressing some of the interests, ideas, or experiences of the individual students—engagement tended to be present. We call this quality Personal Response.

Here, then, are the eight engaging work qualities we isolated and identified.

1. **Personal Response**: The work allows me to react and have my own thoughts. Consequently, there is more than one right answer.

2. **Clear/Modeled Expectations**: I know what success looks like; it has been modeled for me. I know the criteria for my personal response.

3. **Emotional/Intellectual Safety**: I am comfortable taking risks. It is OK to have a different answer or to be wrong on the way to being right.

4. **Learning with Others**: I have the opportunity to interact with others, sharing and analyzing my ideas and theirs. My learning is different because of this process.

5. **Sense of Audience**: Someone whose opinion I care about is going to see my work. I'll be more attentive to my work because of an "elevated level of concern."

6. **Choice**: I get to choose how I am going to gain information or knowledge or how I will demonstrate my learning. I have some control over my work.

7. **Novelty and Variety**: The work grabs my attention because it is new and different. It may be different in procedure, product, perspective, or place.

8. **Authenticity**: I understand that real people need to know how to do this work. I see connections to my world or the world at large.

We then tested these qualities with 5,000 more walks and found that they did, in fact, correlate with student engagement.

Jim: Does anyone ever offer you additions to the list of engaging qualities?

John: I've had that happen a few times. Usually, they feel like we've omitted the engaging quality of Competition.

Jim: Remember when we were in Texas and the middle school football coach made that point?

John: Yes! He said, "Competition engages me. In fact, it's the only thing that engages me." I also remember how you replied.

Jim: I just challenged him to a singing contest. He respectfully declined. It seems that competition is only engaging when you have a pretty good chance of winning.

John: Even so, I think the characteristics of competition that might lead to engagement are covered elsewhere in our list.

Jim: How so?

John: When I compete against others, I am, hopefully, committed to doing my best. I bring my knowledge, experience, and emotions to the table.

Jim: So you have the opportunity for Personal Response?

John: Yes, but not in all competitions. If I am participating in a musical contest, I am deciding how to interpret the selection and make it my own.

Jim: Or a tennis player who is strategizing and responding to the opponent. There's not just one right move; she wins if her Personal Response anticipates the weakness in the other player.

John: On the other hand, in a trivia contest or classroom game of Jeopardy!, there is no Personal Response. The work has to allow for multiple possibilities.

Jim: Here's another quality. If I attempt to perform better because others are watching—other competitors and perhaps even spectators—then I experience a Sense of Audience. And I suppose there might even be the opportunity for Learning with Others.

John: I'm not sure I see that last one.

Jim: Well, in a debate, one participant is responding to another's arguments. There is an interchange of ideas, and one person's thoughts may take a different shape because of what the other said.

John: Maybe, but that's a pretty isolated example.

Jim: I think it may happen more than you think.

John: I disagree. Want to arm wrestle to see who's right?

Jim: No, thanks.

To understand these engaging qualities better and see how they impact student work, let's consider two 2nd grade classrooms involved in the same learning activity, as outlined in the district pacing guide. In the first classroom we visited, Travis shared with us that he was learning "the friendly letter."

When asked what he thought was the most important thing to learn about the friendly letter, he replied enthusiastically, "To have all your parts!"

We asked, "What are all the parts?"

He shot us a look of disbelief. "Don't you know the friendly letter song?" We shook our heads, and his performance began... with singing, hand motions, and choreography.

You have to have a heading   (rubbing his head with both hands)

and a greeting   (waving with his right hand)

and a body   (rubbing his tummy with both hands)

and a closing   (turning around and rubbing his bottom)

and a signature   (signing his name in the air)

(pause)   (catching his breath)

in the friendly letter!"

The performance was impressive, and we walked out of the classroom singing the tune under our breath. We moved on to the next classroom where children were again producing friendly letters—to relatives, friends, and pen pals. This time we spoke to Billy.

"What are you guys doing today?"

"We're writing friendly letters."

"So, what are you learning to do when you write a friendly letter?"

He gave us a puzzled look.

"What's the most important thing to think about as you write a friendly letter?"

"Oh," said Billy. "The most important thing is to be friendly!"

"Okay, so how do you know if you are being friendly as you write?"

"You look at what you are writing and you make sure that you *care* and that you *share*."

"I don't know what you mean."

Billy was excited to teach us: "First, you have to care: 'How ar[e]
do you think about this or that?' Then you have to make sure you[r]
what I'm doing. This is what I think.' Share. Care. Care. Share."

"May we read what you have written?"

"Sure. It's to my grandma."

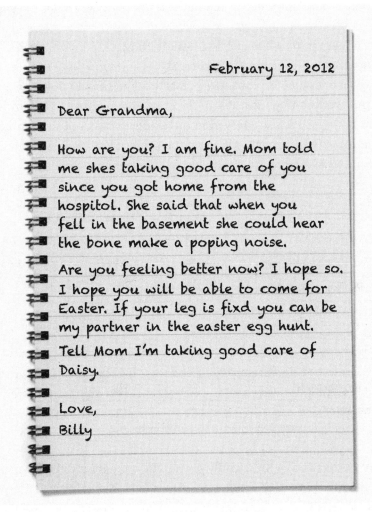

> February 12, 2012
>
> Dear Grandma,
>
> How are you? I am fine. Mom told
> me shes taking good care of you
> since you got home from the
> hospitol. She said that when you
> fell in the basement she could hear
> the bone make a poping noise.
>
> Are you feeling better now? I hope so.
> I hope you will be able to come for
> Easter. If your leg is fixd you can be
> my partner in the easter egg hunt.
> Tell Mom I'm taking good care of
> Daisy.
>
> Love,
>
> Billy

After reading, we had a few more questions for Billy. "Wow, did your
grandmother really break her leg?"

"No, her hip."

"So what are you going to do with this letter now?"

Billy responded in a tone that implied he couldn't believe we did not know the answer. "Um, we're going to mail it."

"Is your teacher going to read it before you mail it?"

"Yeah, but I already know it's a good letter."

"How do you know?"

"Because here's where I shared." He points at spots in the letter. "And here's where I cared." More pointing. "And I have all the parts of a letter." Even more pointing.

"Hope your grandmother gets better soon, Billy."

"Me too. Last year we won the egg hunt!"

Let's pause a moment to look more closely at the friendly letter assignment and view this work through the lens of the engaging qualities. Did Billy experience each of them? Was he engaged in the work? For each of the qualities, decide whether it is entirely absent, might be present but likely won't lead to engagement, or has a strong presence and will engage the learner.

	Absent	Maybe	Strong
Personal Response	☐	☐	☐
Clear/Modeled Expectations	☐	☐	☐
Emotional/Intellectual Safety	☐	☐	☐
Learning with Others	☐	☐	☐
Sense of Audience	☐	☐	☐
Choice	☐	☐	☐
Novelty and Variety	☐	☐	☐
Authenticity	☐	☐	☐

In Billy's class (and in his friendly letter), the content and the purpose seem to matter more than in Travis's classroom, which emphasized the parts of the friendly letter. Personal Response is the starting point for this assignment since Billy is asked to write a friendly letter of "caring and sharing." He chooses to write to his grandmother because he truly cares about what is happening in her life. His matter-of-fact remark about mailing the letter told us that the assignment has Authenticity. Now that we have "bookends" from the engaging qualities, we can look at what else is present.

Clear/Modeled Expectations of purpose (share and care) and structure (all the parts) are evident not only in Billy's product but also in his explanation of what makes his letter a *good* letter. More than getting an *A* or a gold sticker from his teacher, Billy is engaged by a Sense of Audience. He knows that his grandmother will need to read the letter and understand it.

On the framework you've been given, we would probably mark "Maybe" for the quality of Emotional/Intellectual Safety. It's difficult to determine if this assignment was designed to include this quality, but it is likely that writing a letter to your grandmother would offer more opportunity for Emotional/Intellectual Safety than writing to the principal.

There is no Learning with Others here; no other students were involved in Billy's work. Likewise, Choice is not present. Determining the recipient of or audience for the letter is accounted for as part of Billy's Personal Response. There is also no Novelty and Variety in Billy's assignment. This is simply what we do (and what real people do) when we write a friendly letter.

By contrast, the first classroom—Travis's—might have evidence of Novelty and Variety. As we left that classroom, we could not help but smile at Travis's most enthusiastic performance of the friendly letter song. With all of that singing and dancing, surely there must also be engagement. The song, coupled with hand motions, may represent Novelty and Variety, but the engagement is in the song—not the actual writing of the friendly letter. At best, the song serves as a mnemonic device for a letter's parts.

A danger of Novelty and Variety is that it can be self-serving. This quality often shifts the attention from thinking and conceptual learning to the fun and newness of an activity. Do any of these sound familiar?

- Please Excuse My Dear Aunt Sally (order of operations in math procedures)
- Keep Calm At All Sporting Events (levels of Bloom's taxonomy)
- ROY G. BIV (colors of the rainbow)
- Every Good Boy Does Fine (lines of a treble clef)

One could argue that a student who still needs a mnemonic device does not truly understand the relevant concepts.

In processes and products, Novelty and Variety can again override thinking and true learning. A professor of biology shared an example of this issue: "A large percentage of my students have done a squid dissection in middle school. All they remember is dissecting out the pen and writing their names in squid ink. They don't know what the pen is or where the ink sac is located. They know nothing about the function of the structures, but they sure remember writing their names." Science fair projects and shoebox dioramas, for example, may produce this same result if we are not careful.

Let's look at another activity, this one taken from a professional development setting. To model the shift from learning algorithms to "doing math" (Stein, Smith, Henningsen, & Silver, 2009), we often use an activity we call Poster Math. The learners are presented with a problem:

The New Zoo

The city is opening a new zoo!

Altogether, there are 37 animals in the zoo, and they have 118 legs among them. Two of the animals are snakes. None of the animals is injured or imaginary.

What kind of animals and how many of each kind might be in the new zoo?

Participants are asked to start the problem. (In fact, you may want to cover the boxes below, look at the problem again, and see how you might begin.) As they begin to make some progress or commit to an "entry point," we stop them. Selected individuals are asked to stand and transfer their initial efforts to blank chart paper that is hung around the room. We often see things such as this:

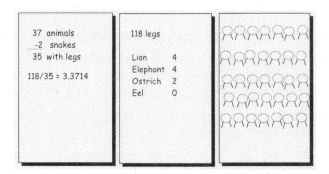

After most participants have committed to a beginning strategy, those still seated are asked to consider each of the posters and go stand by the one that makes the most sense to them. The group at each piece of chart paper is then asked to work together to finish the problem.

(The traditionally calculated answer is 24 four-legged animals, 11 animals with two legs, and two snakes. Usually, though, about five minutes into the groups' work

*time, someone says, "Hey, could there be fish in the zoo?" And if that person says it
loud enough, someone else says, "Oh . . . what about a tarantula?" In reality, there are
an infinite number of "correct" solutions.)*

A spokesperson for each small group shares the group's solution and
describes to the whole group the thinking process they used. Answers and strategies are compared, contrasted, and critiqued.

Do you think it is likely that our teacher participants (or their students
when they take some variation of this activity back to their classrooms) are
engaged? Which—if any—of the engaging qualities do you see in this activity?

	Absent	Maybe	Strong
Personal Response	☐	☐	☐
Clear/Modeled Expectations	☐	☐	☐
Emotional/Intellectual Safety	☐	☐	☐
Learning with Others	☐	☐	☐
Sense of Audience	☐	☐	☐
Choice	☐	☐	☐
Novelty and Variety	☐	☐	☐
Authenticity	☐	☐	☐

Let's consider the qualities as they appear (or don't appear) in the sequence
of the activity. It begins with an opportunity for Personal Response—each
person is encouraged to start solving the problem in his or her own way. An
important part of this approach is that there is no modeling and that expectations are not explicit; Clear/Modeled expectations are not present. (In fact,
modeling would inhibit thinking and limit Personal Response.)

Emotional/Intellectual Safety is part of the task in that each learner may or
may not begin correctly and can rely on the group for help. The small-group
work and associated learner conversations bring about Learning with Others.

The other four qualities are present superficially but with insufficient power
to engage. Although the spokesperson for each group may experience some
Sense of Audience when reporting, it would probably not elevate his or her
commitment to the work. Selecting which chart to stand beside is closer to
Personal Response than to Choice.

The first time this process is experienced in the classroom, students may experience a sense of Novelty and Variety, but that would dissipate quickly. Finally, although some learners may be familiar with zoos and even have an affinity for them, the work itself does not guarantee Authenticity.

Because Personal Response and Learning with Others are such strong components of this activity, it is worthwhile to explore the relationship between the two. Most effective work accomplished in an interdependent group requires that members bring their best ideas and personal views to the table. If the group is truly interdependent and the thinking is genuine, the expressed thoughts of one member will generate reactions and opinions—and maybe even inspire new ideas—among the others. Learning with Others without Personal Response is just a matter of taking turns.

Now that we have inspected both classroom and professional development activities for the qualities, let's take a moment to make this more personal. Think about a hobby or an activity that engages you and what you most enjoy about that activity.

Use the template below to inspect for the engaging qualities:

	Absent	Maybe	Strong
Personal Response	❐	❐	❐
Clear/Modeled Expectations	❐	❐	❐
Emotional/Intellectual Safety	❐	❐	❐
Learning with Others	❐	❐	❐
Sense of Audience	❐	❐	❐
Choice	❐	❐	❐
Novelty and Variety	❐	❐	❐
Authenticity	❐	❐	❐

For most of us, leisure activities provide both Choice and Personal Response. Sometimes, people have trouble differentiating between these two. In general, Personal Response fosters connection, whereas Choice provides control.

The three inspection activities in this chapter are not typical; we were able to find engaging qualities in each of the scenarios. The real world is much different. In 82 percent of the classrooms we observed across North America, we witnessed no engaging qualities at all in the work.

Frequency of Specific Qualities	
Personal Response	7%
Clear/Modeled Expectations	4%
Emotional/Intellectual Safety	< 1%
Learning with Others	5%
Sense of Audience	3%
Choice	2%
Novelty and Variety	4%
Authenticity	2%

Look 2 Learning sample size: 17,124 classroom visits

Two questions we are frequently asked are "How many qualities should my lessons have?" and "How many qualities does it take to engage students?" We answer those questions with data.

- In classrooms where we marked 0 qualities, we never saw engagement. (100% of the classrooms were on-task or off-task.)
- In classrooms where we marked 1 quality, we saw engagement 6% of the time. (94% of the classrooms remained on-task or off-task.)
- In classrooms where we marked 2 qualities, we saw engagement 16% of the time. (84% of the classrooms remained on-task or off-task.)
- In classrooms where we marked 3 or more qualities, we saw engagement 86% of the time. (14% of the classrooms remained on-task or off-task.)

So, how do we design more engaging qualities into our student work?

Like all learners, when we encounter new information or understandings, we make connections between our past experiences and the new ideas. This is a concomitant problem in professional development—we are often asked to

embrace and implement something that is foreign, uncomfortable, and perhaps even counter to our normal practice.

We work with many teachers, schools, and districts that are committed to increasing engagement in classrooms, but they often struggle with where to begin. Schools that have been successful recognize current practice as a starting point. In other words, they look at the current work they are planning for students and inspect it for engaging qualities (just as we did in the previous scenarios). If they find the activity lacking, then they begin to shift practice by "slicing in" a particular engaging quality.

In this often collaborative process, the current practice is tweaked by brainstorming ways to add a single quality. Figure 6.1 (Slicing In Engaging Qualities Tools) provides teachers or professional learning communities with a structure for generating possibilities.

For example, 1st grade teacher Natalie Keorig was considering the math work her students had completed on Tuesday. The students were given a handful of beans and were asked to put three beans in a group on a piece of construction paper. They were then asked to put five more beans in another group on the paper. The final step was to write the number sentence 3 + 5 = 8.

As Mrs. Keorig read through the Slicing In tools, she decided to experiment by adding Learning with Others. In response to the relevant questions on the tool, she redesigned the activity. On Wednesday, students were asked to pull a few beans from the can and place them on their construction paper in a group. They were then told to pull out a few more and make a new group. When this was done, Mrs. Keorig asked each student to turn to a tablemate's paper. The students were directed to look at the new piles in front of them, count the beans in each group, turn that into a number sentence, and record the math on their partner's paper. After they finished, the students returned to their own papers. They were then asked if their partners wrote the correct number sentence.

As her students headed to recess, Mrs. Keorig looked over the work products and found two surprises. Although she had watched Michael record the incorrect number sentence on Natalie's paper, it was now correct—Natalie added a bean to a group to make it so. A second surprise was that two students had chosen to make three groups of beans, and their partners were successful in writing a number sentence with three addends (a skill they had never seen, let alone practiced).

> ### Figure 6.1 » **Slicing In Engaging Qualities Tools**
>
> **Personal Response**
> How can I make multiple answers possible? What can students bring to the activity from their own lives and experiences?
>
> **Clear/Modeled Expectations**
> What do I want students to include in their answers?
>
> **Emotional/Intellectual Safety**
> How can I structure student talk to encourage different, less-obvious, or risky ideas?
>
> **Learning with Others**
> What ideas will students compare or share? How will they explain, critique, or combine one another's ideas?
>
> **Sense of Audience**
> Who (besides me and our class) would be a valued audience for this work?
>
> **Choice**
> What is another activity (or two) that would allow students to learn the same standard yet select between their activities?
>
> **Novelty and Variety**
> What can we do to make this fun, goofy, or different (in procedure, product, perspective, or place)?
>
> **Authenticity**
> What are the obvious real-world connections? Who does this in the real world? How could we simulate the real world in the classroom? How is this represented in the news?

In schools and districts that have focused on a slicing in approach (using this tool), the frequency of student engagement has increased from 6 to 12 percent. This can occur rather quickly. To cross the 12 percent threshold, schools have to move beyond simply slicing in to planning differently. More of the student work—and especially the thinking—has to shift to the learners.

Occasionally, we are asked to rank the qualities—to determine which are the most powerful or lead to engagement most quickly. Those are actually two different questions. Although Novelty and Variety can lead to engagement fairly quickly, there is always a danger that students become engaged in the novelty of the activity and not in the learning (as described earlier). We have no direct data from our visits, but research tells us that Authenticity and Personal Response may be the most brain compatible. When the brain experiences a new situation or is presented with new information, it seeks relevance (Jensen, 2005). In general, this search takes the form of two questions:

- Am I likely to ever need this again?
- How does this connect to what I already know and believe?

The first question seeks Authenticity; the second seeks an opportunity for Personal Response.

To close this chapter, we'd like to ask you to apply what you have learned about the engaging qualities. In his journal entry at the beginning of this chapter, Jerrod was asked to complete an assignment based on a photograph of some footprints. Please inspect Jerrod's description of this work and see if you can identify three or more engaging qualities.

	Absent	Maybe	Strong
Personal Response	☐	☐	☐
Clear/Modeled Expectations	☐	☐	☐
Emotional/Intellectual Safety	☐	☐	☐
Learning with Others	☐	☐	☐
Sense of Audience	☐	☐	☐
Choice	☐	☐	☐
Novelty and Variety	☐	☐	☐
Authenticity	☐	☐	☐

What do you think? Was Jerrod engaged?

Last night I was supposed to do my math homework, but I forgot to draw my "math picture." Since my journal is about my thinking, I THINK I will do some math THINKING now and I THINK I will take my journal to Hansen's class to be graded. My mom actually did my homework for me (sort of).

Unit rate at MY house =

My sister Jessica is going to be in my cousin's wedding next month on Valentine's Day. Last night she put on her dress—the UGLIEST dress ever invented. She looked like a giant pink balloon animal. Mom got mad when I told her that. Dad got mad when he heard how much the dress cost. Then Mom told him it wasn't that expensive. "She can wear it more than ONCE so it won't be so expensive." Jessica cried.

I couldn't believe it—Mom just did my homework!

Mom said Grandma can cut it apart and resew it
so she can get MORE (UGLY) out of it.

Unit Rate at My House

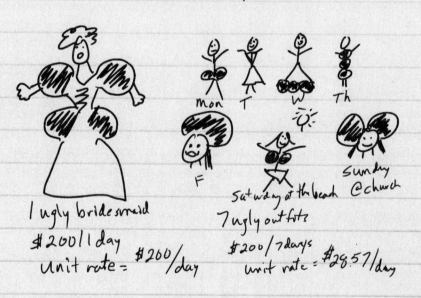

1 ugly bridesmaid
$200/1 day
unit rate = $200/day

$200/7days
unit rate = $28.57/day

Mon T W Th

F

Saturday at the beach

Sunday @church

7 ugly outfits

Instructional Strategies

Jerrod found a way to become engaged with his math homework—perhaps a little bit at his sister's expense. He now seems to have a fairly firm grasp on the concept of unit rate. Let's inspect for the qualities that pulled Jerrod into his homework.

- The work clearly demonstrates Authenticity. Jerrod has taken a very real situation in the household and applied his mathematics lesson to it.
- Jerrod has a sense of Personal Response in his work—he is making the unit rate assignment his own. It's doubtful that there will be too many other assignments submitted with stylish fashion drawings that take us from the church to the beach and back again.
- For a student such as Jerrod, there is also probably a strong Sense of Audience. Mom, Dad, and certainly his sister Jessica will all see these drawings, even before Ms. Hansen, the math teacher, does.

These qualities engaged Jerrod in the work—they grabbed and held his attention—but did they lead to a clearer understanding of the math concept? That seemed to occur specifically with the creation of his "math picture." When Jerrod saw the purpose—*his* purpose—for a nonlinguistic representation, it became meaningful and helped to structure and solidify his learning about unit rate.

Nonlinguistic Representations is one of the categories of strategies described in detail in the ubiquitous book *Classroom Instruction That Works* (Dean, Hubbell, Pitler, & Stone, 2012). In it, the authors report on a meta-analysis that analyzed which instructional strategies have the highest correlation with increased student achievement. Based on an examination of thousands of studies, nine categories of strategies are organized and presented within a framework that is geared toward instructional planning.

Creating the Environment for Learning
- Setting Objectives and Providing Feedback
- Reinforcing Effort and Providing Recognition
- Cooperative Learning

Helping Students Develop Understanding
- Cues, Questions, and Advance Organizers
- Nonlinguistic Representations
- Summarizing and Note Taking
- Assigning Homework and Providing Practice

Helping Students Extend and Apply Knowledge
- Identifying Similarities and Differences
- Generating and Testing Hypotheses

Although specific guidelines were used to identify the effect of these various categories of strategies, we have found through our work that there are some general tendencies that affect the impact of these strategies. In sort, they must be used intentionally, consistently, and correctly.

The first two conditions are fairly self-explanatory. Some strategies are simply more appropriate for certain standards, units, and lessons. For example, if students are asked to compare and contrast two works by the same author or to find the areas of correspondence and distinction between plant and animal cells, then it would make sense to rely heavily on strategies from the Identifying Similarities and Differences category. Also, if these strategies are not part of the teacher's regular toolkit and are infrequently used, then their impact is likely to be negligible.

The third condition—that strategies are used in the right way—has two requirements: the strategy must be in the hands of the student and, in general, at middle levels of thinking or above. For a few of the nine categories of strategies, this stipulation is more applicable than others. However, since our focus is on the learner and his or her behaviors, we feel the distinction is important. Here are the four categories for which the requirement of being in the hands of the student and at middle levels of thinking or above is *not* required for the gains described.

Reinforcing Effort and Providing Recognition: This tends to be a set of tools—used by the teacher—to influence and shape student behavior. Though the teacher may structure opportunities for students to provide some feedback, its orchestration is still within the control of the adult.

Assigning Homework and Providing Practice: Primarily, this speaks to *when* the student work is done. The *Classroom Instruction That Works* authors describe the conditions under which homework has the positive effects desired—one of the most important being timely and appropriate teacher feedback. The work sent home may embody other strategies, but the factors that make it effective in this category are within the realm of the teacher.

Cooperative Learning: Working with other learners can be a powerful motivational tool. (We elaborated on those potential outcomes when describing Learning with Others in Chapter 6.) However, merely working in a social group does not necessarily ensure productive tasks, higher-level thinking, or better learning. We look to high-quality student work for those things.

Setting Objectives and Providing Feedback: Obviously, we think this topic is important—we devoted Chapter 4 to this one strategy. The focus of that chapter, though, is on communicating objectives and helping students personalize them. Setting objectives and providing feedback regarding progress toward them is still, appropriately, in the domain of the teacher.

Jim: If all of the nine categories lead to improved student achievement, then why did we end up focusing on just five?

John: From reading the above, one might think it was by process of elimination, but that really wasn't the case.

Jim: Right. There are positive, inclusive characteristics that describe our group of five.

John: One is that they are all metacognitive.

Jim: Another "meta" word? Meta-analysis and now metacognitive? Are we overdoing it a little with the "meta" thing?

John: It's a perfectly good word . . . and it describes well why these strategies work.

Jim: So, the kids are "thinking about their thinking." Why is that so important?

John: Often when we see these strategies used effectively, the students are as focused on the process as they are on the content. The strategy presents them with a task, and a deep knowledge and mastery of the content is necessary to complete the work.

Jim: The Document-Based Questioning that we described in Chapter 1 is a great example of that. Students were presented with the question "Why did so many people die at Jamestown?" To begin to answer the question, they generated a hypothesis.

John: That's correct. Then they had to glean content knowledge from historical documents to support and test their hypotheses. They really cared more about supporting their claims than they did about specific social studies standards.

Jim: But they learned a lot about Jamestown and Colonial America along the way. They could analyze the information and discuss it fluently.

John: You're describing middle-level thinking.

Jim: And the control certainly was in the hands of the learners.

John: So, how often do we see these strategies implemented with these conditions present?

Jim: Let's look at the data.

Category of Strategies	Learner Control
Identifying Similarities and Differences	2%
Summarizing and Note Taking	4%
Nonlinguistic Representations	3%
Generating and Testing Hypotheses	1%
Cues, Questions, and Advance Organizers	2%

Look 2 Learning sample size: 17,124 classroom visits

As with many of our data sets, teachers tend to be shocked by the low percentages you see here. It is important to remember that these numbers indicate the portion of the school day when these strategies were observed. Lots of other activities—taking attendance, distributing materials, making announcements, transitioning—also take place in the classroom. These data tell us that strategies in these categories were observed between 4 and 12 percent of the time during our visits.

As we will soon see, more than one strategy can be present in a single activity. If all of these were happening simultaneously, which is not likely, then their presence would be seen in 4 percent of the visits—the largest single number seen. If none of them occurred at the same time, which is again not very likely, then we would have seen these strategies in 12 percent of the visits—the total of all of the instances observed.

Of course, one of the most limiting factors of these data is that we only record the strategy when it is in the hands of students and at middle levels of thinking or above. In schools that have implemented the *Classroom Instruction That Works* categories, we often see teachers in front of the class identifying similarities and differences. Alternatively, we might see students reading their textbooks, preparing to memorize lists of similarities and differences generated by the publishers. These would not appear in our data.

So, what do these strategies look like when they're under learner control? Here are some examples from each of our five metacognitive categories.

Identifying Similarities and Differences

In Chapter 3, we talked about one learner-focused tool for identifying similarities and differences: the Venn diagram with lines. Its use facilitates comparing and contrasting, one of four strategies encompassed in this category. The other four are sorting and classifying, creating metaphors and similes, and creating analogies.

We had the opportunity to see a unique use of metaphors and similes when we visited an intermediate school in California. The district had just purchased a new science curriculum, and it was accompanied by a set of DVDs. The 5th grade was studying digestion. We stopped by a couple of classrooms where students, prior to reading the text, were watching a video that showed a cutaway of the human body with the digestive system highlighted. In the first classroom, students sat quietly as the narrator droned, "The food enters the mouth and is cut and ground into fine pieces. Saliva is secreted, which moistens the particles and begins the food's chemical breakdown." On screen, the food is swallowed, and the description continues.

In the other classroom, the sound was turned down, and the teacher had her finger on the pause button. Students watched as the food entered the mouth and was chewed. Just before the food was swallowed, the teacher hit pause.

"What's happening there?" she asked.

"The food is getting chewed up," students volunteered.

"Chewed? What does that mean?"

"Cut into little pieces."

"Does anything else happen in the mouth?"

"Yeah, spit comes in ... well, saliva, really."

"So, in the mouth, at the beginning of digestion, food is cut into small pieces by the teeth, and liquid is added. I want you to be very quiet for 10 seconds and think of something else that works this way. It can't be part of the human body or related to an animal's digestion. Think of another example where something is cut into small pieces and liquid is added. Think; don't talk. We want everyone to have the same chance to think.... Five more seconds.... Now turn to a partner and share your answer."

The responses were varied: a blender, a cement mixer, making soup, and so on. After the partner discussions, students were invited to share with the large group. Each student had to explain the analogy—why it fit, what functioned like teeth, how liquid was added.

"OK, guys, you've heard and generated some great ideas. Which analogy made the most sense to you? It can be yours, your partner's, or another you heard. Which one will help you remember what happens in the mouth? I want you to write it down in your notes—the analogy and the connections. You have five seconds. Commit."

After five seconds, the teacher hit play on the DVD. Students watched as the food was swallowed and rings of muscles pushed it down the esophagus. The process was repeated through each step of the digestive system.

Summarizing and Note Taking

When asked which of the metacognitive strategies is the most frequently observed in U.S. schools, most teachers—and most learners—name Note Taking. We would have to agree. Beginning in 4th and 5th grade, and continuing through higher education, note taking becomes part of the expected classroom routine. This typically looks like a teacher lecturing or displaying a slideshow while the most motivated students transcribe everything and the rest of the class writes only what is preceded by "This will be on the test."

However, this is not the definition of note taking that precedes the powerful effect size described by *Classroom Instruction That Works*. As a category, Summarizing and Note Taking involves so much more than what we just described. At the core of these strategies, Personal Response is the power lever.

During true summarizing, the learner makes conscious decisions about what information to keep, what can be combined, and what is redundant or unnecessary. If the teacher, text, or resource does this for the learner, then the strategy is a nonstarter.

A high school junior in Kentucky told us that "if we all had the same summary in class after reading this text, the text was either too short, too simple, or we don't know why we are summarizing."

In the Common Core State Standards—or the newer, more rigorous standards adopted by your state—summarizing is not the primary verb. It serves as support for a larger question. For example, one 5th grade literature standard is worded like this:

> CCSS.ELA-LITERACY.RL.5.2: Determine a theme of a story, drama, or poem from details in the text, including how characters in a story or drama respond to challenges or how the speaker in a poem reflects upon a topic; summarize the text.

In this case, the skill of summarizing serves to support the analysis and determination of a theme that is predicated upon Personal Response. For example, if one student thinks the theme of *Tuck Everlasting* is "family is all that matters," whereas another thinks the theme is "be careful what you wish for," then they will not pull the same details and plot points to support their ideas. In other words, the students' products—which include summarizing the text to serve a higher cognitive purpose—will be different. They will show that the work was *in the hands of the learners* and at the *middle levels of thinking*.

Likewise, Note Taking is predicated upon Personal Response and making decisions about or connections to content as it is presented or experienced. If every student leaving an AP World History class walks out with the same notes, then this strategy did not occur. The requirement of Personal Response, then, demands that teachers interrupt presentation and delivery with forced mini-tasks of connection, internalization, or clarification.

You can have summarizing without note taking, but you cannot have note taking without summarizing.

In a single-gender classroom in Conway, South Carolina, Angela Jordan had her 7th grade male students take notes as she presented the purpose and function of bones. As she went over a particular function, the boys were each asked to write down the purpose and record her examples. The remaining part of the note-taking organizer was designed for students' Personal Response and connection. Students were asked to draw a picture of something else in the real world that serves the same function. Two of Brandon's answers are shown below.

Function of bone	Examples	My drawing with partner check
Protection- To protect inner organs or delicate tissues	Skull protects the brain Ribs protect the heart and lungs	*helmet is like the bone protecting your head.* Football helmet
Mineral storage- bones are reservoirs for essential minerals for various cellular activities	When the body does not get enough calcium, bones release it to the blood to be taken to muscle cells that need calcium to contract	BANK *I need to make a withdrawal.*

To encourage her students to think through multiple examples and metaphors, Mrs. Jordan also built Learning with Others into the task. When each student had drawn his picture and named it, another student had to explicitly articulate his partner's metaphor. On Brandon's notes, David wrote, "helmet is like the bone protecting your head." At the same time, Brandon turned and wrote next to David's picture of M&M's candy, "the candy shell is the bone protecting the chocolate inside."

This example is similar to the 5th grade digestion activity mentioned earlier in this chapter, and we can use them both to further clarify the strategies. Both the digestion and bone lessons required students to create metaphors (Identifying Similarities and Differences), and both activities forced the Personal Response component necessary in Note Taking.

However, there is a subtle difference: the digestion activity required students to move from a pictorial model from the DVD to a written metaphor, whereas the bone activity began with written information that students turned into pictorial information. This is a nice segue that helps us move into our next strategy.

Nonlinguistic Representations

We've all heard the axiom that a picture is worth a thousand words, and it makes sense. Medina (2008) gave us a similar phrase: "Vision trumps all" (p. 221). No doubt, when a student moves or translates information from a linguistic form into a visual image or kinesthetic interpretation, the potential to store the information is dramatically increased. Memory—consisting of linguistic and nonlinguistic storage—is increased when the two come together during the learning experience.

For example, a few bars of a song can instantly bring forth images of where we were when we first heard it or cause us to see in our mind's eye the face of a dear friend from the past. Somehow in our brains, the lyrics and perhaps the tune itself are linked to that face or place deep within our memory.

As a result of our classroom visits, we have come to believe that the category of Nonlinguistic Representation is actually broader than simply moving from words to pictures (or vice versa). It occurs anytime the brain works in one language and moves to another. Content and disciplines typically have a "preferred language." When students can demonstrate an understanding of a concept outside of that language, the brain is focusing on the patterns of the content and not the just the knowledge (Asher & Adamski, 2009).

For example, the language of instruction in an elementary music class involves pitch, notes, and rhythm—all of which are about sound. With this in mind, when an elementary teacher in Connecticut wanted to make sure his students understood the concept of *crescendo*, he told them, "I want you to get ready. We are going to act something out that we've been learning about, but this time, there will be *no music*. You cannot make a sound. Instead, you must show me what my idea *looks* like using your hands or your bodies. Remember, no sounds. The word is . . . *crescendo*."

Immediately, students began to use their hands—spreading them apart or reaching from the floor up into space. Other students crouched into little balls and then slowly stretched their bodies to a full, standing position. One student scrunched up his face and then raised his eyebrows.

"Great. I saw that everybody showed me a soft or quiet volume. Show me again how you did just the soft volume. . . . Stop! Look at all the way our friends showed soft volume. Now slowly increase your volume. . . . Great! Now show me the last part of a crescendo—full volume. The next word is going to be easy: *decrescendo*. Go!" Without a word or a sound, the students reversed their crescendos.

"Now it's gonna get tricky. We're going to learn a new word: *sforzando*. This is when a sound crescendos very quickly and then decrescendos, but remains. Think about that for a moment. Now, without making noise, show us what that looks like." As the students tried out their nonlinguistic representations, the teacher was able to ask the class whose representation showed all three parts of a sforzando.

Finally, the students were given a starting pitch and asked to demonstrate each of the three dynamic changes by combing their kinesthetic movements and the original language of the discipline—sound.

As we have worked across North America, we've seen lots of evidence that various initiatives were trained with enthusiasm only to be abandoned. One of the few programs we have seen with staying power is Thinking Maps (see www.thinkingmaps.com). If the critical elements of Personal Response and middle-level thinking are a part of the activity, then graphic organizers—just like all of the strategies we have discussed thus far—are highly effective at getting students to "see" their thinking and the organizational patterns in information. Recall the Venn diagram with traits (lines) from Chapter 3 and notice how Jerrod's thinking changed as a result.

As we have seen, though, Nonlinguistic Representations has more possibilities than just graphic organizers. In an effort to make the mathematics in her 7th grade class more meaningful, Mrs. Jergensen asked her students to describe a situation represented by the following expression:

$$5(2a + 3b)$$

When her students began to work in the language of numbers to simplify the expression, she stopped them. "No, I don't want you to simplify the expression; I want you to come up with a real-life example."

Most of the students then began to write explanations of how to simplify the expression. "First, you say, 'five times the first number in the parentheses and...'" They moved from the language of numbers to words, yet they remained fixated on the *steps* of the procedure.

Frustrated, Mrs. Jergensen asked her student to draw a picture of something that could be written with the expression. The students struggled for a bit, but they began to propose and draw scenarios, such as "A mom is putting together lunch bags for each of her five children. She puts two apples in each and three bananas in each. How many pieces of fruit should she buy?"

An interesting discussion followed as the students could see that the distributive property "shows" 10 apples and 15 bananas, which totals to 25 pieces of fruit. A second conversation was about the inaccuracies of adding the variables *a* and *b* in the abstract. The students decided that "how many pieces of fruit" was a misleading question. It was authentic but not mathematically appropriate. In the end, they landed on "What fruit should she purchase?" as a better question. The valid struggle to conceptualize was enhanced by the non-linguistic strategy.

Generating and Testing Hypotheses

Of all of the *Classroom Instruction That Works* strategies, Generating and Test-ing Hypotheses may be the one that most requires a shift from teaching to learning. The first verb in this category invites analysis—finding patterns in the information before you. Even though the teacher or text may assemble infor-mation in front of a student, it is the student who must find a pattern in the information. Inquiry learning is predicated upon this part of the strategy. The second verb asks learners to explore further and see if the patterns continue or give the expected result. This strategy is recorded in our data when either part is at the center of student work.

In a 1st grade classroom, Mrs. Viala was telling a story to her students on the carpet. The story she told was her own loose interpretation of *The Enormous Watermelon* (Parkes, Smith, & Davy, 1986):

> *Little Miss Muffet planted a watermelon seed that grew and grew and grew into a long, lush watermelon vine. At the end of the line, a small watermelon began to grow. And it grew and it grew and it grew until it was an enormous watermelon.*

Little Miss Muffet wanted to eat the watermelon, so she went to pull it out of the garden. She pulled and she pulled, but she could not lift it, for it was an enormous watermelon. The first day she called a friend, Little Jack Horner, and together they pulled and they pulled, but they could not lift it, for it was an enormous watermelon. The second day she called her friends Jack and Jill, and together they pulled and they pulled, but they could not lift it, for it was an enormous watermelon. The third day she called her friends the butcher, the baker, and the candlestick maker, and together they pulled and they pulled, but they could not lift it, for it was an enormous watermelon. The fourth day...

Mrs. Viala stopped. "Boys and girls, I forgot what happened on the fourth day. When you go back to your tables, I want you to draw a picture of what happened that day. I know that many of us will want to solve Little Miss Muffet's problem, and that would be nice. But that's not what I want you to do. What I want you to do is find a pattern you heard in our story and extend that pattern. We'll share these when we come back from lunch."

When the students shared their pictures, Marissa's picture showed her extension of the pattern as she explained to the class, "So the next day she called even more friends and they pulled and they pulled but they could not lift it. It was just too big!"

Viala asked, "What pattern did Marissa hear?" Many students answered that she had more people help. Others said that they "pulled and pulled."

Sean's picture was hard to decipher, but it obviously had four characters on it. "Four" was all he offered as an explanation. As some of the students snickered, Mrs. Viala refereed. "Sean, I think your answer makes perfect sense. Tell us all how you got to your answer."

"Well, the first day one person came. On the second day, two people came. On the third day, three people came. So... four."

Jose then shared his picture. "The giant came down the beanstalk, and he just picked it right up!"

"Uh oh," cried a child on the carpet. "He solved her problem."

"Yes, but I think he heard a pattern, too. Jose, what part of your picture shows the pattern? And what part is the solution?"

Jose was clear. "Another story person came to help. That's the pattern. He was a strong giant. That's the good part—they got to eat the watermelon."

Our 1st graders explain this strategy well—the answer is secondary to the logic of the patterning. It really doesn't matter if you think any additional characters will suffice or if you think it has to be a nursery rhyme character. Each of these answers is predicated upon an articulated pattern. We may not agree with one another's answers, but we cannot deny the logic or evidence upon which they are based.

Earlier, we said that specific disciplines have specific languages. Likewise, the strategy of Generating and Testing Hypotheses is known by different names in different subject areas. Here are some examples:

- Mathematics: estimation, establishing reasonableness, problem finding
- Literature/Reading: prediction, inference
- Science: experimental inquiry
- Social Studies: systems analysis, market analysis

In a 5th grade math classroom, a teacher gave the following scenario, basically asking students to test three hypotheses for reasonableness:

> Michael claims that if you add three fractions, then your sum can never equal the number 3. Javon says that's not true and that he just did it on his paper. Carol claims she can add three fractions and end up with a number bigger than three. She did it yesterday and found a sum of 5. Choose one of your classmates and prove his or her hypothesis.

Most students proved Michael correct by adding proper fractions:

$$\frac{1}{2} + \frac{1}{2} + \frac{1}{2} = 1\frac{1}{2}$$

or

$$\frac{99}{100} + \frac{99}{100} + \frac{99999}{100,000} \neq 3$$

becaus less than 1 + less than 1 + less than 1 = less than 3

Others proved Javon correct:

$$\frac{2}{2} + \frac{3}{3} + \frac{4}{4} = 3$$

A few proved Carol's hypothesis:

$$1\frac{1}{2} + 1\frac{1}{2} + \frac{4}{2} = 5$$

Some students may have chosen which claim they thought was correct and then worked backward to develop mathematical proof of their thinking. These students are perhaps more deductive in their approach. More inductive learners may not have known which claim was true but began to try out three possible fractions until they arrived at a claim they could prove.

Let's look at another scenario. A history class has been studying the rights guaranteed in the First Amendment of the U.S. Constitution—religion, speech, press, assembly, and petition. As a final task in the unit, the students worked in groups. Each group had to choose and remove two of these basic rights. With the remaining rights intact, they had to decide how the following events might have been affected:

- Martin Luther King Jr.'s "I Have a Dream" speech on the National Mall
- *The Washington Post* uncovering the Watergate scandal
- Women gaining the right to vote
- An all-night prayer vigil in memory of a fallen soldier
- The creation of a website that details the sources of politicians' campaign contributions

Clearly, there are hundreds of possibilities, but the students all quickly realized that the rights work together to provide the life—and the history—we all know.

One of the saddest things we see in classrooms is when an otherwise successful Generating and Testing Hypotheses activity is stopped cold by students' conditioned need to identify the "right" answer.

Cues, Questions, and Advance Organizers

You may know this one by another name. Other models based on this foundation sometimes use the phrase *activating prior knowledge*. Regardless of the name, the intent is the same—students make Personal Response connections to content or concepts in advance or in anticipation of upcoming instruction. They need not know where the lesson is going for this moment of learning to be powerful. In fact, we have found that the action of posting an objective prior to this moment of student response often reduces students' flexibility and depth of thinking—along with levels of student volunteerism—as the learners try to guess the teacher's predetermined answer.

When in the classroom, we look for this strategy as an anticipatory set. This verbiage harkens back to Madeline Hunter's elements of an effective lesson (1994), but *anticipatory* may still not provide the clarity we want. According to various dictionary entries, two extreme phrases that demonstrate the positive and negative nature of anticipation are as follows:

- to realize beforehand; foretaste or foresee: *to anticipate pleasure*
- to nullify, prevent, or forestall by taking countermeasures in advance: *to anticipate a military attack*

To be clear, we hold that the design and implementation of an anticipatory set should actually cause students to want *more* of the content, not *dread* it.

In an 8th grade classroom in Washington state, a teacher started class with two things written on the board:

1933   Alabama

"I want each of you to jot down in your notebooks a list of five possible traits or descriptions of people who lived in this time and in this place. Write whatever you think."

After students completed their lists, they were reconfigured into groups of four. The students were then asked to share their traits and categorize them as "positive, negative, or neutral." They began sharing their traits and even argued over whether a trait was positive, negative, or both positive and negative. They remained completely unaware that the teacher was moving through the room, distributing paperback novels.

"OK, 1933. Alabama. The novel is by Harper Lee. It's called *To Kill a Mockingbird.* I want you to read the first chapter tonight and be prepared to share where you found evidence of one of your group's traits. I want you to tell us if your perceptions were right or wrong and show where in the novel you found that information."

Although the qualities of the activity—timing and task—make this a moment of an anticipatory set, the students were also generating hypotheses about southerners. The text and conversations about the narrative should allow for rich discussions that *test* these hypotheses. When we asked one of the young men in class what the objective for the activity was, he replied, "She hasn't told us yet, but I bet we just did it."

We've worked with a number of school districts across the country—large and small—that initially became enamored with *Classroom Instruction That Works.* District leadership was convinced that if we (as a profession) could just get this one thing right, then student achievement would soar. They directed lots of resources toward this end. The results were rarely spectacular.

There appear to be several reasons for this breakdown. High on the list may be patience and persistence. We rarely give initiatives enough time to have the desired impact. A list of professional development topics is published, training is conducted, and next year we move on to a new list. In one of the districts where we did see some progress, the superintendent said, "Let's commit to this for at least five years. There are nine strategies; we'll concentrate on one each semester and help teachers build their toolboxes." All went well for two years. Then the superintendent took a job with another district and the new leader came in with his own set of priorities.

Like any initiative, a strong groundwork must be laid. Most of the teachers with whom we work have valuable teaching experiences and have arrived at a set of strategies they believe to suit their content, their students, and themselves. Before asking them to change, does administration take the time to explain why a new method will be more effective (and ultimately more rewarding) than a "time-tested" one? Are growth and positive change accepted as a valued and expected quality among all professionals?

Another important prerequisite for success with these strategies is that they—the strategies themselves—first must be taught. This works best when ✈

they are introduced outside of a content area and with ideas familiar to students. Understanding how a tool or process works is crucial before attempting to use it with new learning. This type of frontloading can be hard for teachers. Pacing guides often encourage us to be efficient rather than effective.

As you probably understand, nine categories of strategies encompass a lot of new ideas. The biggest may be embodied in the teaching-learning shift. As students become more invested in their work and take ownership of it, we will begin to see learning improve and resultant achievement gains of the kind predicted in *Classroom Instruction That Works*.

 As a form of Summarizing, please complete the 3-2-1 activity below.

Three separate words that are important for you concerning this chapter:

1. _____

2. _____

3. _____

Two questions you still have:

1. _____

2. _____

One simile:

These strategies are like _____,

because _____.

Law and Order

Supreme Court Docket #492179 (Chung! Chung!)

This is my story:

Mrs. Garcia is not here today because she went to a workshop for teachers. If she was here this never would have happened. If she was here there would not have been a substitute with a World War II DVD.

Mr. Diemer said we were supposed to watch the horrible video and take notes. It was just a bunch of black and white scenes of history with some old guy telling what he thought and talking over the good parts. So when they were showing Roosevelt with his cigarette, we heard the old guy instead of the president. I thought everybody should know what Roosevelt said, so I just stood up and did my best impression. "We have nothing to feah, but feah itself!" Mr. Diemer said "shut up and sit down." I don't think teachers should talk that way.

When they showed Churchill, I did not STAND UP. I just said, "We shall fight on the beaches, we shall fight on the landing grounds, we shall..." And Mr. Diemer said, "I'll not tell you again!" But he DID tell me again when I was in the middle of doing my best General McArthur stepping off the plane. That's when he sent me here. He said, "take your things and go to the principal's office."

Mrs. Menendes, when I got here, your secretary said you were in a meeting and that I should sit here and think about what I had done until you could see me.

I decided to write up my account of what happened (like on Law and Order). Not Guilty! (Chung! Chung!)

I don't think I should be in trouble and there's no need to call my mom. She's already worked up about my cousin's wedding tomorrow. If Mrs. Garcia was here, she would have liked the way I "made it my own."

8

Differentiation

Primary Student Activity by Grade Cluster		
Grade Levels	Activities Involving Listening/Watching	Identical Seat Work
All Classrooms (PreK–Grade 12)	49%	26%
Primary (PreK–Grade 2)	37%	44%
Intermediate (Grades 3–5)	43%	28%
Middle School (Grades 6–8)	52%	18%
High School (Grades 9–12)	63%	15%

Look 2 Learning sample size: 17,124 classroom visits

John: What do you see in this data set regarding student activities in the classroom?

Jim: Even before that, I think we have to talk about what we *can't* see.

John: What do you mean?

Jim: I think we have to make the point that these data aren't good or bad. To use a trite phrase, it is what it is.

John: You're exactly right. Students can learn some important lessons by observing and can get valuable practice from uniform seat work, including worksheets.

Jim: But we also know the power of having students actively do work they perceive as personal and relevant. That would not be included here.

John: Right. So, with that clarification, what do you see in the data?

Jim: Our kids are listening a lot! And the amount of time actually increases as they are promoted from grade to grade.

John: I think part of the reason for that may be developmental. I'm not sure you could keep a 6-year-old in a chair, listening, for 63 percent of the school day.

Jim: I believe there may be another reason, too. Secondary teachers love their subject matter and want to share it. The most efficient way to do that is to talk about it.

John: You're a great example of that. You taught theater and don't hesitate to share your love of it with others—even if they are not as interested.

Jim: And yes, Mr. Science Teacher, we love your thrilling insights into the periodic table of the elements.

John: Well, it *is* interesting.

Jim: To you. Which may also describe why the percentage of time spent on identical seat work declines. The presentation of information is seen as more important at the secondary level.

John: While at the elementary level, the emphasis is on skills rather than information. Skills require practice, thus more uniform seat work.

Jim: Notice that at all levels, the total time spent on these two categories is between 70 and 81 percent. If we subtract housekeeping tasks, announcements, interruptions, and transitions, it doesn't leave much time for learners to complete personalized, relevant tasks.

John: How can teachers shift some of that time, make learning more personal, and not drive themselves crazy trying to manage it?

Jim: And thus begins Chapter 8.

Carol Ann Tomlinson (2014) describes differentiated instruction as instruction that is responsive to student readiness, interest, and approach to learning. When teachers understand their students as unique learners and plan work to meet their individual needs, preferences, and interests, the classroom is responsive rather than uniform and static.

We agree wholeheartedly with Tomlinson's choice of the word *responsive* and celebrate her description. In fact, we have found that in classrooms that have made the shift from teaching to learning, the very nature of the shift causes differentiation to occur.

Consider this simple example from the kindergarten carpet. After reading *The Three Little Pigs* to her students, Mrs. Carter asked a comprehension question (actually knowledge/recall) of her students: "What did the third pig use to build his house?"

All of the successful students answered, "Bricks!" The expectation was that the story would teach "brick" as the correct answer and the learner would repeat it.

In another kindergarten classroom, Miss Howard follows up her reading with a question of Personal Response: "Which of the three little pigs do you think was the smartest and why?" This question requires analysis (finding patterns that demonstrate smartness) and leads to evaluation (using a pattern to support a judgment).

Bethany explains, "The third little pig is smartest cause he built his house all out of bricks."

"How does that make him smart?"

"The bricks were strong, and the wolf couldn't blow it down, and the pigs were all safe."

Damien disagrees. "I think the first pig was smartest because he didn't have to work too hard making a brick house."

"Do you think some people might say he was just lazy?"

"Maybe, but straw is easy and didn't take too long, so he finished fast and got to play his fiddle with his brother. That's smart."

Malcom adds to Damien's idea. "He was also smart because when the wolf blew down the house, he knew how to get to his brother's house."

"What kind of smart is that?"

"He knows how to stay alive!"

Rather than simply assigning "right-or-wrong" feedback, Miss Howard's follow-up questions are responsive and personal to each of the learners. Differentiation has occurred.

In many schools we visited, differentiation was their current initiative, yet they struggled to get the desired results because they asked teachers to manage something akin to a three-ring circus. The reason they struggled is that they had not yet made the shift from teaching to learning. It is, after all, impossible to teach in 28 different ways simultaneously. However, with knowledge, training, and appropriate lesson design, it is possible to facilitate the individualized learning of 28 different students.

How, then, do we design for differentiation?

Tomlinson identifies four classroom elements that provide opportunities for the modification of learning activities: content, process, product, and learning environment. Because it is primarily in the realm of the teacher's control and management, we are not going to consider learning environment in this chapter.

Content Differentiation

Educators use the word *content* to mean many things. We will need to define— or at least clarify—some terms in order to avoid confusion.

- *Concept*: a big idea, usually described in standards and curriculum documents
- *Skill*: behavior involving retrieval of information, rules, or steps
- *Vehicle*: that which provides access to concepts or skills

All three of these words are used as synonyms for *content*, but let's look at an example to understand the distinction between each component.

- Concept: finding figurative language
- Skill: by decoding the words
- Vehicle: of a Langston Hughes poem

We do not believe that concepts should be differentiated. In terms of content, we believe that the vehicle should be differentiated in order to make concepts more accessible to all students. Therefore, we will postpone our discussion of differentiation of skills until Chapter 9.

If we return to the previous example, we want all of our learners to be able to identify and appreciate figurative language. Some of our students may not be able to decode the words used by the poet Langston Hughes. Therefore, we may need to find an alternative passage to serve as the vehicle.

Process Differentiation

Process refers to the learning tasks and cognitive actions our students use to understand and make sense of information, ideas, and skills. Although process differentiation encompasses many options and learning formats, for sake of example we will consider *tiered* or *parallel tasks.*

In a 4th grade classroom in Kentucky, Mr. Gedding presented two problems to his students. "Select one of the two problems to solve. You may work alone or in small groups. When I call time, you will need to explain what you have

LEAD 21
Unit 5–communities
– could be used for
reading response

done and what you have figured out. If you don't quite have an answer, that will be OK. We'll look at what we have. If you finish one and want to work on the other, that would be OK, too."

Choice #1	**Choice #2**
In a group of people, each person shakes hands with each other person exactly once. How many handshakes will there be if there are three people? Four people? Eleven people?	Look at the following patterns. How many dots will there be in the tenth picture?

Very quickly, the students set to work. Some of the students began to act out shaking hands and recording their results. Others worked independently and produced imaginary guest lists, drawing lines that connected each guest to the others. A tally sheet of handshakes was the strategy employed by one lone mathematician. One young man filled a page of paper very quickly with dots in triangle configurations, whereas two girls worked together to write a series of numbers—1, 3, 6, 10—and the question "What's going on?" One group of three students quickly solved Choice #1 and moved on to Choice #2.

One thing certainly rings true in this classroom—every brain is wired differently. By presenting parallel tasks, Mr. Gedding brings about process differentiation as students make initial decisions about which task "makes more sense." Students who are more visual in their approach may gravitate toward Choice #2, since it might be more readily accessible, whereas our more kinesthetic learners might start acting out Choice #1.

This technique of implementing parallel tasks is espoused by Marian Small (2012). Allowing learners to select the task and an entry point into the task is already a richer experience for individual students. Bringing the whole class back to a comparison between the tasks reinforces the learning. (By the way, the patterns in the two problems are identical: 1, 3, 6, 10, 15, 21...)

Let's look back at the bell-ringer activities from Chapter 5 (see pages 70–71):

• In the Dickens activity, will learners approach and answer the task in different ways, based upon schema, experience, and preference?

- In the manifest destiny activity, is there evidence that a student who does not yet have mastery of the concept is still given a "forced opportunity" to make connections to what he or she *does* know?
- Finally, would the math problem presented allow for students to attack the situation through a variety of strategies?

If the answer to these questions is *yes*, then each of the tasks incorporate process differentiation.

Product Differentiation

Students demonstrate their mastery of learning outcomes by producing things. Differentiation of product describes the various artifacts we are willing to accept as evidence that the desired knowledge or skills have been successfully acquired. The choice may be the teacher's or—if engagement is valued—the student's. A school story will show us what product differentiation can look like in practice.

In one Texas classroom, the 5th graders had just finished studying the various regions of the country and were ready to begin the obligatory state report.

The teacher said, "Boys and girls, we've studied the different parts of our country, and we have learned a lot! Now you are going to have the chance to become an expert on one state. We'll research on the Internet, of course. The school library has books on all of the states, and our classroom library has some atlases and almanacs. In the top drawer of my filing cabinet are fifty file folders, one for each state, filled with travel brochures.

"Now, I would like for you to pick your state. Which state would you like to learn more about so you can become our classroom expert? There's only one other rule. Since, as a class, we already study a lot about Texas, I'll ask you not to select that one."

(Please note that this would be a rare case where the content is differentiated but the standard is not. We already have a fair bit of differentiation with the selection of "my" state. If you are looking for engaging qualities, this is probably an act of Personal Response rather than Choice, even though students are asked to choose a state. Personal Response is about making a connection; Choice is about control. Indeed, there was probably a connection that motivated many state selections. For example, perhaps a student used to live there, vacationed there, or has a relative who lives there.)

After the students had shared the states they wanted to study, the teacher continued. "That sounds great! We each have a state to learn about. A couple of you chose the same state, but that's OK. Our goal is to learn how to gather, organize, and evaluate information. After you have done that, you will have the opportunity to share it with the class.

"There are several ways you can do this. If you would like to write a report and summarize it for us, you can certainly do that. If you would like to create a presentation, that would be fine, too. If you would like to write and sing a song about your state, that would be fun. Last year, someone made a state quilt. A few years ago, a student made a mobile. You could create a travel brochure or a set of postcards that come from that state. If you're good with technology, you could design a state website. In fact, if you have other ideas about how you would like to share your information, I'll listen to those, too."

(Here we see a great example of product differentiation. Not only do students have choice in how they will present their information, but, most likely, they will opt for methods of presentation with which they feel competent, providing a degree of Emotional/Intellectual Safety. In general, process differentiation allows for Personal Response; product differentiation offers Choice.)

"Whatever method you use to share your information, it must include the following: the name of the state, its capital city, the region of the country in which it is located, the state's major cities, its population, and its main industries. Along the way, I'm sure you'll find other interesting information you'll want to share with us as well." The teacher then distributed a rubric and a reflection sheet for the state report—delineating how points would be earned for the organization of content and evaluation of information gathered—as well as product parameters.

(Thus, design of the work incorporates another engaging quality, Clear/Modeled Expectations. If viewing this assignment through the lens of effective strategies, all students will participate in summarizing and note taking as they gather and organize information. Some may, by virtue of their product choice, create nonlinguistic representations, identify similarities and differences, or generate and test hypotheses.)

With Personal Response, you get to decide your answer to the question. With Choice, you get to decide on the question.

As we mentioned in Chapter 4, one result of the shift from teaching to learning is that learners become fluent in the thinking required of particular disciplines. Tasks that differentiate process are more likely to develop this fluency. In other words, if the work we plan for kids allows them to approach a task the way they would naturally think through a situation, then we build individual thinkers, not just repeaters.

We have to look closely, then, at the work we plan for our students to see if the task will differentiate the thinking process. In mathematics, one tool that will help us analyze the nature of the work is found in Figure 8.1. The Task Analysis Guide is a tool developed by Margaret Schwan Smith and Mary Kay Stein (1998) to help teachers inspect their task design for thinking and cognitive demand. They classify mathematical tasks into four categories: memorization, procedures without connections, procedures with connections, and doing mathematics. The first two categories operate at lower levels of cognition, whereas the latter two require higher levels of cognitive demand.

As an exercise, consider the two math problems from Mr. Gedding's 4th grade classroom. Using the characteristics within the four quadrants of the Task Analysis Guide, find the appropriate placement for the two tasks.

If we look at the tasks and the way a group of learners would approach the tasks, we see that they fall into the higher-level demand of doing mathematics. As our students demonstrated, "there is not a predictable, well-rehearsed approach or pathway explicitly suggested by the task."

Another way to look at the tool is through the lens of process differentiation. Memorization tasks and tasks that require procedures without connections do not play a role in process differentiation. (By contrast, they may be involved in content differentiation.) Because Personal Response is required as individual students make connections to or find their own unique entry points into the problem, the tasks of procedures with connections and doing mathematics will bring about process differentiation.

As much as we value tools such as the Task Analysis Guide—or Bloom's taxonomy, for that matter—we must add two caveats or cautions. The first is about implementation. As teachers ourselves, we have found that we sometimes design great tasks of higher cognitive demand only to "overteach" them and remove the rigor during implementation. The TIMSS data presented in Chapter 1 suggest that we are not alone in this practice.

A second caveat is this: lower levels of thinking and tasks of lower cognitive demand are neither bad nor undesirable. On the contrary, much success in life

Figure 8.1 » **The Task Analysis Guide**	
Lower-Level Demands	**Higher-Level Demands**
<u>Memorization Tasks</u> • involve either reproducing previously learned facts, rules, formulas, or definitions OR committing facts, rules, formulas, or definitions to memory. • cannot be solved using procedures because a procedure does not exist or because the time frame in which the task is being completed is too short to use a procedure. • are not ambiguous—such tasks involve exact reproduction of previously seen material and what is to be reproduced is clearly and directly stated. • have no connection to the concepts or meaning that underlie the facts, rules, formulas, or definition being learned or reproduced.	<u>Procedures with Connections Tasks</u> • focus students' attention on the use of procedures for the purpose of developing deeper levels of understanding of mathematical concepts. • suggest pathways to follow (explicitly or implicitly) that are broad general procedures that have close connections to underlying conceptual ideas as opposed to narrow algorithms that are opaque with respect to underlying concepts. • usually are represented in multiple ways (e.g., visual diagrams, manipulatives, symbols, problem situations). Making connections among multiple representations helps to develop meaning. • require some degree of cognitive effort. Although general procedures may be followed, they cannot be followed mindlessly. Students need to engage with the conceptual ideas that underlie the procedures in order to successfully complete the task and develop understanding.
<u>Procedures Without Connections Tasks</u> • are algorithmic. Use of the procedure is either specifically called for or its use is evident based on prior instruction, experience, or placement of the task. • require limited cognitive demand for successful completion. There is little ambiguity about what needs to be done and how to do it. • have no connection to the concepts or meaning that underlie the procedure being used. • are focused on producing correct answers rather than developing mathematical understanding. • require no explanations, or require explanations that focus solely on describing the procedure that was used.	<u>Doing Mathematics Tasks</u> • requires complex and nonalgorithmic thinking (i.e., there is not a predictable, well-rehearsed approach or pathway explicitly suggested by the task, task instructions, or a worked-out example). • requires students to explore and understand the nature of mathematical concepts, processes, or relationships. • demands self-monitoring or self-regulation of one's own cognitive processes. • requires students to access relevant knowledge and experiences and make appropriate use of them in working through the task. • requires students to analyze the task and actively examine task constraints that may limit possible solution strategies and solution. • requires considerable cognitive effort and may involve some level of anxiety for the student due to the unpredictable nature of the solution process required.

Source: From "Selecting and Creating Mathematical Tasks: From Research to Practice," by M. S. Smith and M. K. Stein, 1998, *Mathematics Teaching in the Middle School, 3*(5), p. 348. Copyright 1998 by the National Council of Teachers of Mathematics. Reprinted with permission.

is predicated upon recall and "knowing the steps." Many teachers we work with have asked, "Do you have a task analysis guide for science or social studies?" Sadly, we have not taken the time to build these. We do, however, find that teachers can very quickly take the Task Analysis Guide for mathematics and place other content across the four domains.

We encourage you to consider your own curriculum now and see if you can think of content examples—skills or concepts—that you would want in each of the categories named by Smith and Stein. What do you believe learners should have at the automatic level of memorization? What procedures do you want your learners to have and trust—even if they don't understand how they work? What connections do you want your learners to see (and find for themselves) in the content? What types of activities require "doing science" or "doing art"?

The idea of differentiation is often presented as a tool or protocol that separates and sorts learners based on their abilities—in other words, easier for these learners but more challenging for those. This may be the unfortunate consequence of seeing it from the teaching perspective. Our interpretation of Tomlinson's work involves finding the right match between student and vehicle, letting students find their own ways of accessing and processing information and then determining how they will demonstrate understanding. We see differentiation as a chance to increase engagement and thinking for all learners.

To facilitate the learning of 28 different students, a teacher does not need to become 28 teachers. Rather, the work he or she plans should allow the 28 students to own their learning.

Now let's think outside the box. Aside from an educator…

1. Who would have a use for the information presented in this chapter?

_____

_____

2. Why would they want this information?

_____

_____

3. How would they use this information?

_____

_____

I'm sitting in my new math class today. Why am I in a new math class? Because the teachers had some PLC. I don't know what that means, but Mrs. Garcia said we were going to swap some teachers and kids based on our math benchmark tests.

So I've been in Mr. Jackson's class this week. At first I thought it was because they thought I was dumb in math. Mr. Jackson said that our group needed to look at new ways of learning about probability because we might have some confusion. Michael is in my regular math room right now working on ratios with Mrs. Hansen, but I'm already good at that.

At first, I didn't like changing my math class, but Mr. Jackson does the probability different and it makes more sense to me. (Sorry Mrs. G, but even YOU said that's why we were doing this!)

I actually like it now. I even finished early and decided to do my journal while we wait to go back to our regular class.

9

Learning Pathways

> *The only thing we can be sure about with "thumbs up" is that they have thumbs.*

It has been said that assessment distinguishes between teaching and learning (Fisher & Frey, 2007). In other words, the content may have been "presented," but assessment reveals whether the desired knowledge and skills were acquired by the learner. Of course, in this age of accountability, testing and assessment have taken on many implications and shades of meaning—not all of them positive. In the cloud of sentiment whirling around externally imposed testing, it is easy to lose sight of the power of well-designed classroom assessments. From checking for understanding to end-of-course examinations, the forms of assessment can be as varied as their purposes.

Richard Stiggins (2007) has developed a helpful framework for describing and classifying assessment activities. He uses the label *assessment of learning* for quizzes, tests, final papers, presentations, and other culminating or summative activities. These are the methods that come most readily to mind when considering the point made by Fisher and Frey above. At the end of the learning process, we need some tool to help us answer the question "Did they get it?"

Assessment can occur during the learning process. It can take the form of questioning, written work, technology, or any other tool that gives the teacher formative feedback on each student's progress. Stiggins refers to this as *assessment for learning*. A key component is the concept of self-assessment. Ideally,

127

student and teacher act in tandem, determining current levels of mastery, areas of deficit or excellence, and appropriate strategies for addressing both.

In our L2L classroom visits, assessment of learning is fairly easy to identify. We note assessment for learning when we see students involved in evaluating their own learning. We may also see them being given information by their teacher that, going forward, would alter the learning process.

(Please note that under these definitions, "Everyone got it? OK? Let's move on then" would not qualify for inclusion in our data as assessment for learning.)

Purpose of Assessment	
Assessment of Learning	10%
Assessment for Learning	3%

during

Look 2 Learning sample size: 17,124 classroom visits

In his early years as director of curriculum and instruction in the Sheridan School District in Arkansas, John was leading the elementary schools through a very difficult change in math instruction. Various teachers throughout the district were piloting a new mathematics program (and philosophy) that required students to answer and solve math problems in numbers, pictures, and words.

To evaluate the learning—as well as the impact of the pilot curriculum—all students in the district were given benchmark assessments at regular intervals throughout the year. Potential test questions were gathered from released items from the state proficiency exam and from teachers across the district. In order to make the test more secure, however, only John composed the actual exams. John sent the following problem to 1st grade classrooms across the district for the spring benchmark:

> 14. Four dogs and four cats walked two blocks to the park. Show your work.

Obviously, he forgot to proofread. On the day of the benchmark testing, the phone in the district office rang continuously. "John, item number 14 does not have a question. What should I tell the students? How should I handle this?" Following the model of the state testing protocol, John replied to each and every teacher, "Just tell the kids to read it again and do their best."

When the benchmarks were scored, a very interesting trend came to light. In traditional classrooms, the students left question 14 blank or wrote simple number answers—0, 4, 16—with the answers 8 and 10 being the most frequent. In the pilot classrooms, the numbers, pictures, and words gave us great insight into students' thinking.

One very interesting response came from Emma, who wrote this as her explanation:

$$
\begin{array}{r}
4 \\
4 \\
+2 \\
\hline
10
\end{array}
\qquad
\begin{array}{r}
4 \\
4 \\
-2 \\
\hline
\end{array}
$$

↖ The anser is 10. ↑
becus this is legel.   This is elegel

The scoring committee spent a solid hour dissecting and hypothesizing about Emma's response. What was she trying to tell us? Had she learned that the presence of three numbers in a problem could only lead to addition as a possible solution? After all, how many times are children asked to subtract a long series or columns of numbers? Perhaps Emma was struggling with the unnamed concept of integers. How could you subtract 4 from 4 and then subtract 2 from 0?

Though the primary intention of the benchmark was assessment of learning, it ultimately became assessment for learning. For the remainder of the year, we designed and implemented a series of math problems with more than two addends and more than two subtrahends. Assessment is important, but what we do after we assess is even more important.

(For the inquiring minds that need to know, the original question should have read "If four dogs and four cats walk two blocks to the park, how many paws went to the park?")

John: Let's talk about RTI for a few minutes.

Jim: Yuck! Respiratory tract infections? I had one of those when I was a kid. They are nasty!

John: No, silly. Response To Intervention.

Jim: Oh. That makes a little more sense.

John: We see the phrase used in lots of schools that have professional learning communities, but it has always been a little problematic to me.

Jim: I did some reading about it the other day, and things became much clearer.

John: Explain, please.

Jim: Do you know the model that is most commonly used to identify learning disabled students?

John: The discrepancy model. We look at a student's abilities as described by a standardized test, then look at his or her achievement levels. If there is a significant difference—or discrepancy—the child may be identified as learning disabled.

Jim: Exactly right. Except some people believe that isn't very scientific—that other factors could enter in. There is some subjective judgment involved, too. So, according to William Bender and Cara Shores (2007), some in the special education field proposed Response To Intervention as a better identification model.

John: Go on.

Jim: When students struggle in the classroom, they are provided with scientifically based interventions. Their response to these interventions—which have been shown to be successful with other kids—determines whether they are identified as learning disabled.

John: So, now that special-ed model has been adapted from its original purpose and used to describe changes in instructional programs for a much wider range of kids.

Jim: Exactly.

John: This may answer another question we have always had.

Jim: Which one?

John: Do you remember the four questions proposed by Rick and Becky DuFour and Bob Eaker (2008) as critical to the work of professional learning communities?

Jim: What is it we want our students to know?

John: How will we know if they are learning it?

Jim: How will we respond if they don't learn?

John: And what will we do if they are already proficient? Do you see anything missing?

Jim: Powerful initial instruction!

John: Yes. Perhaps that's why RTI (emphasis on the *I* of *intervention*) became the popular model for student support.

Jim: What if RTI was Response to Instruction? That would be a more inclusive term, wouldn't it?

John: I think so.

Jim: And I'll bet we can provide stories, ideas, and structures to help make some of those connections.

John: Let's start with this school story.

At Jack Jouett Middle School in Albemarle County, Virginia, the School Based Intervention Team (SBIT) was originally formed to discuss student interventions. The traditional model of an SBIT includes teachers and interventionists who meet when a child is struggling in school. Leadership at Jouett found that this model limits perspective and ownership of the process. Principal Kathryn Baylor decided to expand the SBIT process to include all teachers in a grade level (rather than just the respective student's teachers), as well as counselors and interventionists, to broaden the sharing of ideas and develop staff capacity for implementing classroom interventions.

During the first few years of this process, Principal Baylor noted that teachers tended to focus on the symptoms, rather than the root causes, of each student's learning problems. These symptoms generally manifested as distracting or off-task behaviors. In addition, the team consistently passed responsibility for the interventions to people "outside" the classroom. By contrast, Baylor believed that these symptoms could best be addressed by improving instruction inside the classroom.

The Jouett leadership team also recognized and articulated a number of other factors that had undermined their efforts:

1. Behavioral problems are symptoms of academic problems. The team often wants a specialist to treat these symptoms rather than address academic issues in the classroom.

2. Outside interventions are actually separating students from the situations they need help confronting and overcoming.

3. Classroom teachers are already doing everything they know how to do.

The Jouett teams reworked their Intervention protocols dramatically, expanding the professional capacity of the staff. The teams now work cohesively across a grade level. For example, when a 6th grade student is referred, all of the 6th grade teachers are present to help plan the intervention—regardless of whether or not they teach that student. The counselors prepare a summary page of the student's benchmark scores, common assessments, attendance, and other important data. The student's actual classroom teachers begin by sharing the child's strengths with the larger group before identifying specific problems or issues. The whole group then begins to brainstorm a menu of in-class strategies, ideas, and interventions that the student's core teachers can implement. Before the group disperses, an action plan is developed for each of the classrooms involved, the teachers select from the options presented, and a date is set to revisit and reflect on the student's growth. Outside help comes only after the grade-level teachers have implemented interventions and then reported back to the team on their effectiveness.

The large number of classroom teachers involved in this process increased the quantity and quality of strategic ideas—it was a true professional learning community. To make the process even more efficient and effective, Jouett staff also used technology to plan, implement, and reflect on the classroom interventions.

Figure 9.1 shows the extensive list of in-class activities and strategies the faculty has developed over time. Each of the line items is a live link to a series of possible strategies, which are housed on the school's shared drive. If the group recognizes that a student's attention span is providing challenges to instruction and learning, then they might choose to focus on strategies for "chunking assignments/assessment." This link would then redirect to a separate list of nine strategies for how to actually implement and incorporate this skill in classroom procedures (see Figure 9.2). The shared drive also allows teachers to quickly record which strategies were tried, the dates they were tried, and their varying degrees of success.

While the adults in the building are quite proud of their intervention model, Principal Baylor admits that it was painful for a few years. It took a while to build capacity and trust among faculty members, administrators, and the rest of the intervention team. Schoolwide interventions and special services are still necessary for some of the students at Jouett, but many more students are developing the skills they need to be successful while remaining in the classroom.

It is interesting to note how this list of interventions reads like a series of best practices for any classroom.

Figure 9.1 » **Menu of Interventions**

Academic Performance	Academic Behavior	Social/Emotional Behavior
☐ After-school Study Hall ☐ Chunking Assignments/ Assessment ☐ Conference ☐ Differentiation ☐ Extended Time ☐ Fluency Screenings and Practice ☐ Frequent Checks for Understanding ☐ Literacy Strategies • Before • During • After ☐ Parent Contact ☐ "Peer Buddy" ☐ Preteaching of Content Vocabulary ☐ Reteaching Strategies ☐ Schedule Change ☐ Seating Change ☐ Small-group Pull Out ☐ Study Guides ☐ Support with Graphic Organizers ☐ Tutoring	☐ After-school Study Hall ☐ Assignments ☐ Behavior Contract ☐ Conference ☐ Copies of Notes ☐ Extended Time ☐ Frequent Checks for On-task Behavior ☐ Homework Folder ☐ Monitor Long-term Progress ☐ Organizational Support ☐ Parent Contact ☐ "Peer Buddy" ☐ Seating Change ☐ Self-monitoring Checklist ☐ Study Skills and Test-taking Strategies ☐ Teacher Mentor ☐ Work System (To-do List)	☐ Alternative Classroom Meeting ☐ Behavior Contract ☐ Breaks ☐ Conference ☐ Detention ☐ ESSS Referral ☐ Frequent Checks for On-task Behavior ☐ Giving Student a Leadership Role ☐ Hallway Supervision ☐ Loss of Privileges ☐ Parent Contact ☐ "Peer Buddy" ☐ Referral to Counseling Office ☐ Seating Change ☐ Self-monitoring Checklist ☐ Teacher Mentor

The interventions at Jouett Middle School have provided some wonderful results for students. However, as we know, schools and their resources can differ widely. How might we operationalize and replicate some of these concepts across schools with varying resources, schedules, support systems, and structure?

Let's first agree that learning is a process—a journey, if you will. As with most journeys, it begins with our current location (present state of knowledge and skills) and continues to a destination (an enhanced level of knowledge and skills). True to the journey metaphor, any of several paths may successfully lead to our desired destination. For the purposes of our graphic organizer (see Figure 9.3), let's think of that journey as moving from left to right across the page.

Figure 9.2 » Example Submenu of Interventions

Academic Performance	Academic Behavior	Social/Emotional Behavior

☐ After-school Study Hall
☑ Chunking Assignments/
  Assessment
  ○ Assignment Given Section
    By Section
  ○ Assignment Given Page
    By Page
  ○ Project Broken Into Individual
    Steps
  ○ Test Breaks
  ○ Test Given One Page at a
    Time
  ○ Test Given Section By Section
  ○ Writing Assignments One
    Paragraph at a Time
  ○ Writing Assignment Given
    in Stages
  ○ Other: _____
☐ Conference
☐ Differentiation
☐ Extended Time
☐ Fluency Screenings and Practice
	☐ After-school Study Hall
	☐ Assignments
	☐ Behavior Contract
	☐ Conference
	☐ Copies of Notes
	☐ Extended Time
	☐ Frequent Checks for On-task
	  Behavior
	☐ Homework Folder
	☐ Monitor Long-term Progress
	☐ Organizational Support
	☐ Parent Contact
	☐ "Peer Buddy"
	☐ Seating Change
	☐ Self-monitoring Checklist
	☐ Study Skills and Test-taking
	  Strategies
	☐ Teacher Mentor
	☐ Work System (To-do List)
		☐ Alternative Classroom Meeting
		☐ Behavior Contract
		☐ Breaks
		☐ Conference
		☐ Detention
		☐ ESSS Referral
		☐ Frequent Checks for On-task
		  Behavior
		☐ Giving Student a Leadership Role
		☐ Hallway Supervision
		☐ Loss of Privileges
		☐ Parent Contact
		☐ "Peer Buddy"
		☐ Referral to Counseling Office
		☐ Seating Change
		☐ Self-monitoring Checklist
		☐ Teacher Mentor

Along the way, we may have to stop and ask ourselves, "Where are we now?" On our learning voyage, we'll call these "assessment points." They may take the form of tests, quizzes, portfolios, performances, reflections, or even information shared by members of a child-study team (such as the one operating at Jouett). These assessment points can identify a fork in the road. With this in mind, consider the following road map.

The process originates with an assessment point. Before instruction begins, it is useful to understand each student's current level of knowledge regarding the content. We all recognize the value of preassessment, but it is a step that is often omitted or forgotten in classroom practice. Moving forward, armed with these diagnostic data, we are ready to proceed to what this book is about—designing lessons that are learner-focused, engaging, cognitively demanding, and effective. (It's a truth not often considered: more successful initial instruction will lead to the need for fewer interventions.)

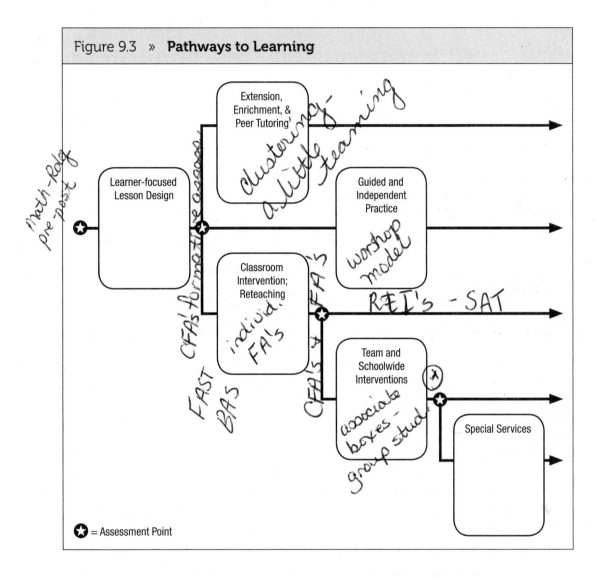

Figure 9.3 » **Pathways to Learning**

After this, there is another assessment point. Did the students reach the desired level of learning? This question may be answered in one of three ways.

- **Yes.** The student has demonstrated mastery of the intended content. At this point, he or she may proceed to *extension* (access to new concepts) or *enrichment* (deeper learning on these concepts) or may be asked to provide *peer tutoring* help to other students.
- **Yes, but...** The student has shown knowledge of the desired content, but needs further support. This can take the form of *guided or independent practice.*

- **No.** The student has not yet successfully acquired the necessary knowledge or skills. The next step is *reteaching* or *interventions within the classroom.*

Of course, this last group of students provides us with a unique set of challenges. Most likely, in our initial planning, we chose the methods that we thought had the best chance of providing access to the content for all students. When that doesn't work, we tend to repeat the same lesson but louder and slower—if we have time to reteach at all.

When Jim taught high school language arts, one of the courses he was assigned had an unfortunate title: *Freshman Non-College-Bound English.* Most of the students were males, and most had repeated the class at least once. One day in mid-September, one of his students stopped by Jim's desk after class.

"Mr. G., why do we have to read the same stories we did last year?"

"Well, you didn't learn what you were supposed to, so you'll have another chance."

"Yeah, I know. But if it didn't work then, what makes this year any different?"

Rather a haunting question, no? That's especially true when one considers the learning outcomes. We weren't supposed to be teaching "The Scarlet Ibis." We were supposed to be using that short story to teach about figurative language and plot structure. If the reading level presented too great a challenge, why couldn't we have used a different text to help students access those literary structures and conventions—for variety's sake, if nothing else? Again, Medina (2008) tells us that our brains pay attention to vision, patterns, and emotion. When repeating the content, something needs to "feel" different for our minds to reengage.

A teacher may, after exhausting his or her own set of strategies and tools, turn to colleagues for thoughts and guidance. This is the true power of professional learning communities. In this way, the pathway among classroom intervention, reteaching, and team and schoolwide interventions can form a loop (as it did at Jouett). The classroom teacher turns to colleagues for new ideas and then tries them in his or her classroom. Eventually, with more assessment point data, the student may actually participate in interventions provided in another classroom or an alternative time or setting. Finally, when we—as reflective, flexible, collaborative professionals—have exhausted our resources, our students may need the support and structure provided by special services.

This instructional movement within and across classrooms requires a schoolwide dedication of resources—not the least of which is time.

In schools where this has become a natural part of practice, it becomes, well, *natural.* A number of years ago, we were conducting an instructional audit of an urban school just a few days before the winter/holiday break. The principal was accompanying us on the visits, and as we headed down the primary-grades hall, she was proud to tell us that the school was all about instruction and that they had no time "for fluff"—even around the holidays.

When we entered the first kindergarten classroom, our eyes were drawn to a young girl intently concentrating on her task. She was meticulously cutting out a strip of red construction paper, which she then carefully looped and glued together around a green link of a long chain. The principal tensed up a bit as we moved over to the chain-maker.

"What are you working on there?"

Without skipping a beat, the child responded, "I'm making a one-to-one correspondence chain with an *AB* pattern!"

"What's a one-to-one correspondence chain?"

"It helps gives us something to really count like this." As she pulled the chain from the floor, she began to touch each of the links. "One. Two. Three. Four. See, that's one-to-one." She dropped the chain back to the floor and added, "But this is *reciting* your numbers: one, two, three, four, five. You're just saying them in order, but you're not really counting anything."

"Cool. So what's an *AB* pattern?"

She looked at us as if we were in need of real help. "A, B, A, B... What comes next?"

We nodded, "OK."

"No, I'm really asking you. A, B, A, B... What comes next?"

"*A!*" one of us said.

"See, you already knew what it was."

After we chuckled to ourselves, we asked, "So why is it important to learn this?"

"Well, you have to know your patterns. You have to be able to cut and glue. And you have to be able to count to 100. And since it's Christmas, I picked red and green paper." She paused for just a moment. "We have to practice these things, but mostly it's so Miss Butler can work with the small groups on different reading stuff."

As we reentered the hallway, the principal cleared her throat nervously. "What do you think about that?"

We almost spoke over each other. "Well, *everybody* is clear about the priority of the small group and the purpose of independent practice." It is remarkable how quickly our learners figure out what matters in school.

 In keeping with the assessment theme, write a test question that would assess a major concept in this chapter. The question must require cognition greater than recall.

_____

_____

_____

BELL RINGER (IN YOUR JOURNAL):
CSI ON "PAUL REVERE'S RIDE"

COLOR–THAT CAPTURES THE BIG IDEA

SCENARIO–A PICTURE OF SOMETHING
THAT HAPPENS IN THE TEXT

ICON–A SYMBOL OF THE
BIG IDEA OF THE TEXT

CSI "Paul Revere's Ride"

C: Black—the "black hulk" threat of the British man-of-war and the black river on which it might sail toward the blackness of the dark, unprepared houses.

S:

I:

10

Closure

In her book *Mastery Teaching* (1994), Madeline Hunter describes the seven parts of a logical, well-designed lesson plan. One of the elements she describes is closure, an intentional summary of what was done and covered in the lesson. Because Hunter's model speaks primarily to instructional planning, closure is most often viewed from that perspective.

- "So, in summary, boys and girls, today we..."
- "You should keep in mind these three big ideas from today's lesson..."
- "Some things you should remember for the test are..."

Of course, if we are making a shift from teaching to learning, the focus of closure—in whose hands the control and thinking lie—will have to change.

 Patricia Wolf and Viola Supon (1994) help us begin to see what this transformation might look like. They tell us, for instance, that for closure to be effective, students must be "active agents" in summarizing and analyzing what they have just learned. It occurs during a short period of time, most often no more than four to eight minutes. Though it usually occurs at the end of a lesson, it may be used at any time when it is necessary to reinforce or clarify key concepts. By eliciting this feedback from students—*all* students—teachers are also able to conduct a final "check for understanding" as we discussed in Chapter 9.

 In a school in southern California, we entered a 6th grade classroom in the middle of math and approached a group of students who were all writing in black-and-white composition books. One of us asked, "What are you guys doing today?"

Derrick happily replied, "Oh, we are writing in our workbook."

We were confused. There were no workbooks on the table—just the composition books. "OK, so what math are you working on in your workbook?"

"We're not doing *math* right now; we're doing our *workbook*."

We were still confused. "I don't see a workbook," John said.

"Well, our workbook is not about math. Every month, each of us chooses a career we might be interested in. We read about it and do some research, but every now and then, Mrs. Patton will stop us in the middle of whatever we are doing—math, social studies, or science—and she just yells 'Time to go to work!' That's when we get out our workbooks and write how our career would use whatever we are learning."

interesting idea!

"Ohhhh. So what is your career?"

"I'm a professional baseball player. This week in math we've been practicing converting between fractions, decimals, and percents and going back and forth. So I have to tell why a baseball player would need to know this and how he would use it."

"And how would he use it?"

"Well, in baseball, you might only get a hit one out of every five times at bat, but you would never say that your batting average is one out of five or 20 percent. You have to put everything into decimals in baseball. That would be a .200 batting average—probably good enough to keep you on the pro team. It's above the Mendoza line."

"Wow, you know a lot about baseball. And math. Is everybody in class doing baseball?"

Derrick looked around the room and pointed. "Allison is doing something about being an architect."

"Hi, Allison. Why would an architect need to know how to convert these numbers?"

"Well, if you were measuring something in inches, the tape measure is only marked into eighths, but when you calculate length, you'd be better off to use 0.125 inches. You would use percents when you're calculating cost overruns. If you use the metric system, it's so much easier."

Effective closure activities will have a variety of correct answers, thus our belief that *Closure is a final moment of Personal Response.* How often do we see closure that meets these conditions? Let's take a look.

Closure (all grade levels)	
Students involved in personal activities of closure	< 1% (11 times)

Look 2 Learning sample size: 17,124 classroom visits

True, we were not in the classroom at the end of the lesson for all 17,124 visits, but we were there during the final minutes of a substantial number of them. For instance, if we view a lesson as taking approximately 40 minutes and if our four-minute walks occurred randomly, then we were in the classroom at the end of the lesson for 10 percent of the visits—about 1,712 times. The eleven instances where we observed "students involved in personal activities of closure" are less than 1 percent of *that*. Keep in mind that closure can be designed to occur during the lesson as well.

John: Why do you think we see student-controlled closure so infrequently?

Jim: I think a big reason is that teachers just run out of time.

John: There is the pressure of the pacing guide with all that material to cover.

Jim: Interestingly, the dictionary defines *cover* as "to obscure from view."

John: You know what I mean. There is also the student-controlled piece of your question. If, as a teacher, I have just a few minutes left, I may find time to summarize what we did but not facilitate an activity of student summary and reflection.

Jim: ✳ That sort of takes us back to the efficient versus effective dichotomy. What I can do quickly and proficiently...

Impt//

John: . . . may not lead to the deepest and most long-lasting results.

Jim: Do you remember that middle school we visited where they took on the time and closure issue?

John: I do. They first let the kids know that the bell didn't end the class—the teacher would let them know when class was finished.

Jim: Then they set the bell to ring five minutes before the end of class. The signal didn't release students; it let the teacher know that it was time to begin closure.

John: Without some signal like that, the closure we usually see is "Close your books; it's time to go home."

Jim: If closure is so valuable, then why isn't it a part of our regular practice?

John: Maybe we should have our readers reflect on that.

Jim: At the end of the chapter.

Looking back at the previous nine chapters, we have already provided seven activities of closure that can easily transfer to K–12 classrooms. What follows are brief descriptions to remind you of each of these activities. For more detail, please revisit the closure of each chapter.

Chapter 2: *Continuum.* Students are asked to place ideas, facts, or concepts in an evaluative order.

Chapter 3: *Make and Support a Claim.* Rather than making a simple restatement, students develop an argument about an idea from the information and recognize the counterargument.

Chapter 4: *In the Voice of...* Students think through the content from a different perspective and develop a product that explains the concept to a given audience.

Chapter 5: *Four Rs.* Students restate, react to, remember, and respond to content ideas.

Chapter 6: *Treasure Hunt.* The new content and concepts become "look-fors" as students inspect their past work or other models.

Chapter 7: *3-2-1.* Students select three important words from the learning, two questions they might still have, and create one simile. Teachers can substitute other short tasks in this structure.

Chapter 8: *In the World.* Thinking outside of school, students articulate who else might use this information, why they would need the information, and how they might use it.

Chapter 9: *Test Question.* Students write a test question to assess a major concept of the lesson. Open-ended questions can be shared with the class or a partner.

Conclusion doesn't mean "ending."

There are scores of closure activities designed to elicit the personal response and connections we want for our learners. Some of the favorites we've seen—or developed ourselves—are included here. Many can be used without any direct instruction of the associated techniques or strategies, whereas a few might take a moment of explanation to ensure the activity is "worth the time" and elicits the appropriate thinking required in closure.

Four-student Summary. Each student writes a single word from the content that is meaningful to him or her. In groups of four, students then share, compare, and contrast their words. The final task is to write a connection among the four words or a proper, accurate sentence that uses all four words. If all four of the words are the same, then students must explain why.

Exit Ticket. Students are asked to write and then post or turn in a short note that explains the main idea of the day's lesson or—perhaps more important—their reaction to it, a personal connection to it, an example of it, or a question about it. Aside from this personal response, a second intent of the exit ticket is for students to have an opportunity to "speak" to their teacher about the learning. Students should be encouraged to let their teacher know what help or additional information is needed.

Summaries R Us. In a combination of the Four *R*s activity and the exit ticket, students are given strips that allow them to choose which reflective summary technique they use—restate, react, remember, or respond with questions. As seen in the example below, this task requires students to identify which technique they are using, making the task more metacognitive.

Date	Concept/Idea	restate react remember respond with questions
10/22	Two types of imperialism—regressive and progressive	Even if a country thinks they are approaching something progressively, wouldn't the other country or colony still see it as regressive?

Post Card to an Absent Student. Each student uses an index card or sticky note to explain the main ideas, steps, or concepts learned in class to someone who did not hear them. Instead of just writing "Hi, Mike... Here's what we learned in class today," students are encouraged to explain why the new curriculum might seem hard or tricky. Other possibilities are to include how the content is similar to or different from something they've already done.

NEWS. This mnemonic device reminds students to write four thoughts about the content in question: What else do we *need* to know? What *excites* you? What is *worrisome* (the downside to the idea)? What is your *stance* or opinion on this topic?

Three Cs. Students write a personal *connection* to the information, a *challenge* within the content or to the information, and a description of how the information *changes* what they know or think about the content.

I Used to Think/Now I Think. Rather self-explanatory in title, this activity requires students to complete both of the phrases and describe how the lesson changed their thinking.

Headline. Students write a newspaper headline that captures an important idea of the lesson. Asking students to write headlines about the same information but for two different sources—for example, a traditional newspaper such as *USA Today* and a "tabloid" such as *The National Enquirer*—adds a bit of novelty. In a variation, a high school social studies class could be asked to write the "screen crawls" that appear along the bottom of two television news shows: one conservative and one liberal.

Seven-word Summary. Working in pairs or groups, students are asked to write a summary of the information in a complete sentence of exactly seven words.

Tweet Me. Students are allowed 140 characters to capture or react to the lesson or content. This can be done on paper or—more authentically—in the twitterverse.

Shaping My Thinking. Using different geometric shapes, students record their responses:

- Square: *How does the new information square with what I already know?*
- Triangle: *What are three points to remember?*
- Circle: *What questions are still circling around my brain?*

Sentence, Phrase, Word. Working toward increasing brevity, students write a sentence about the core idea, a phrase that moved or provoked them, and the most powerful word in the content.

Two additional closure activities will be introduced in the final chapters of this book.

As we close the chapter on closure, we ask you to repeat the CSI format that Jerrod used in class for "Paul Revere's Ride." Feel free to revisit Jerrod's journal entry for an exemplary model of student response.

CSI. Choose a *color* that captures the big idea of this chapter and explain the connection. Next, draw a *scenario* of this chapter. Finally, draw an appropriate *icon* to symbolize the chapter.

Well, it's kind of funny that today is Friday the 13th, since it's my last day in this school—except I'm not laughing. I've seen the house we'll be living in and it's not bad. I even met some kids at the skateboard park near my new school. It will probably be okay. At least I'm not crying and acting like it's the end of the world like Jessica is.

Hey, Mrs. G, I know I'm supposed to be writing today about what we read last night, but I figure it's my last day and you won't mind. I'm going to leave this in my desk, so you might even read this. (Did you see how I used my its and it's correctly? You're welcome!)

Really, though, I want to thank you for a great year. You know I like history, but I never really liked reading so much until this year. I hope my new teachers will be cool.

I think I learned a lot this year, so even if the new school is not great, I should be okay. Hope a new kid moves into your class to make it fun like I did. Anyway, thanks!

We have nothing to feah, but feah itself!

11

Reflection

Professionals, by definition, have the responsibility to grow and change. As knowledge in the profession develops, so should resultant practice. Although this growth may culminate in action, it finds its origins in reflection. As John Dewey said, "We do not learn from experience.... We learn from reflecting on experience" (Dewey, 1933, p. 78). In our work, we have long recognized the need for reflection. Successfully facilitating it, however, has certainly been a learning process.

In our early work with classroom walkthroughs, we presented feedback to individual teachers as a reflective question. There were several preconditions involved in the writing and delivery of this question:

- First, of course, it had to be in the form of a question. (This was to help remove preconceptions and judgment.)
- The question had to be delivered in person—orally—and not in writing. (Much meaning in communication can be lost without body language, tone of voice, eye contact, and so on.)
- The feedback had to be shared within 24 hours. (After several days, it would have lost meaning and relevance.)
- The exchange had to occur in a neutral place. (We didn't want it to feel like teachers were being "called to the principal's office" with all that that implies.)
- When writing the question, the word *you* was to be avoided. (It might make the receiver feel singled out or defensive.)
- Finally, after the question was asked, the teacher was not allowed to answer it—at least not immediately. (Reflection takes time.)

Can you figure out why that feedback model didn't work very well? As good as our intentions were, there were so many barriers embedded in the process that it almost precluded reflection from occurring. In addition, the overwhelming requirements of the structure (intentionally) removed emotions and relationships from the process. A message that could have been shared easily and openly between two trusting professionals became stilted and artificial.

Throughout this process, we learned some important lessons:

1. We are emotional *and* rational creatures. Feelings, passions, experiences, and data all inform and advance reflection.

2. Reflective processes must be natural in content, timing, and setting.

3. Participants need a degree of separation—chronologically and emotionally—from the practices being considered.

As we sought to learn more about effective reflective practice, we discovered the work of Jennifer York-Barr, William A. Sommers, Gail S. Ghere, and Jo Montie (2001). Their mnemonic device (Figure 11.1) helps define and clarify the conditions and actions that promote reflection in professional practice.

A worthwhile goal for a school or district is the development of a culture in which reflective practice is the norm. York-Barr and colleagues contend that this can best be accomplished through a sequence of four stages of reflection: individual, paired, small group/team, and schoolwide. Although there is certainly a logical progression to this framework, we have found the reverse is often much more effective in practice. First, create conditions that promote and support reflection within the school. As a faculty, use reflective processes to consider data and solve problems. Then create opportunities for PLCs, departments, and grade-level teams to think, process, and act together. Next, allow educators to work together in pairs, committing to shared deliberation and application. Finally, permit and expect individuals to use reflective practice to guide and shape their actions and interactions.

John: The work of Jennifer York-Barr and her colleagues has certainly advanced the cause of reflective practice.

Jim: I especially like the mnemonic device in Figure 11.1. It really helps explain what reflection looks like and how to support it.

John: Of course, there are a couple of lines included on which you and I still don't quite see eye to eye.

Jim: Inside-out, Outside in?

Figure 11.1 » A Mnemonic Tool for Reflecting on Reflection

*R*elationships are first

*E*xpand options through dialogue

*F*ocus on learning

*L*eadership accelerates reflective practice

*E*nergy is required for any system to grow

*C*ourage is needed to reflect and act

*T*rust takes time

*I*nside-out

*O*utside-in

*N*urture people and ideas

Source: From *Reflective practice to improve schools: An action guide for educators* (p. 153), by J. York-Barr, W. A. Sommers, G. S. Ghere, and J. Montie, 2001, Thousand Oaks, CA: Corwin. Copyright 2001 by Corwin. Reprinted with permission.

John: Exactly. As a science teacher, I know that behavior is a matter of stimulus and response. Seen through that lens, all reflection is outside-in.

Jim: Well, Mr. Wizard, do you agree that some people are more reflective than others?

John: Certainly.

Jim: Follow me here. I drive by a sign for a funeral home. I think, "Life is so short... relationships are precious... I haven't talked to my sister in ages... I think I'll call her tonight." And I call her.

John: It's still outside-in. Seeing the sign was the stimulus. You just had a convoluted response.

Jim: You are so frustrating!

John: When you know I'm right.

Jim: I know we can find common ground on this. What if we look at the direction of the *impact* of reflection? Sometimes, my environment and the people around me may cause me—after some reflection—to change my beliefs and actions. Outside-in?

John: Yes, and I think I see where you're going with this. My beliefs may change—again through reflection—inspiring me to actions that may actually change my environment and those around me.

Jim: Inside-out!

John: I suppose so, but it all still starts with a stimulus.

Jim: You're impossible.

John: Perhaps the scientist in me wants to bring analysis into the reflective process.

Jim: Let's explore the similarities and differences between the two.

Reflection and analysis may appear on the surface to be very similar processes—since they are both about identifying our thoughts. We will consider analysis further in Chapter 12, but let's take a moment to discriminate one from the other. Reflection is typically an emotion-based process. It draws on past experiences, feelings, and beliefs. By contrast, analysis is a process based on vision and truths. One person's analysis should be confirmable as true if others look at the same information.

To illustrate the difference (and to appease John's argument of outside-in), let's consider an exercise of Reflection and Analysis that we often use when we are presenting or training in schools. The two of us are known to wear colorful neckties, and we may ask teachers to tell us "five things you think or notice about Jim's tie." The following responses demonstrate reflective answers:

- I like it!
- It's rather loud.
- I love the blue… it brings out the color in your eyes.
- It looks expensive.
- It looks cheap.

These are examples of reflection. Each is predicated on a past belief—the person already likes blue or finds paisleys to be garish. In other words, they could be argued based on each person's preferences.

Other responses move toward the analytical:

- It has dolphins on it.
- There is a diagonal stripe.
- It's long enough to cover your belt buckle.

These are examples of analysis. Each of the statements is based on something that can be seen "right there" and can be verified by anyone else in the room simply by looking at Jim's tie.

In a mathematics PLC, "Our incoming freshmen are weak in math" is a very different thought than "72 percent of our 8th graders scored *below proficient* in simplifying algebraic expressions." Whereas the analytical statement of data may seem like a more likely starting point for action, we've found that the reflective step actually begins to move people. To maximize our professional growth (both individual and collective), schools need to honor and even activate reflection as separate from analysis.

For one year of his life, John taught kindergarten. He was not trained as a kindergarten teacher, but his K–12 gifted certificate rendered him "qualified enough" when a kindergarten teacher went out on maternity leave the day before the school year began. It was quite a year of learning!

At the same time, John was taking a graduate class taught by Joseph Hart, one of the founders of the American Psychodrama Association (now the American Society of Group Psychotherapy and Psychodrama). Dr. Hart had pioneered psychotherapy techniques designed to accelerate patients into articulating and accepting the realities of their current situations through a set of activities that involved acting and drama. The intent of these techniques was to get a patient to dig deeper into his or her understanding of self and the surrounding world—a truly reflective process—but at a faster pace than traditional psychiatric approaches.

As he made a personal connection to his current teaching assignment, John decided to try some of these techniques with his kindergarten students to see if 6-year-olds could be more thoughtful and reflective in their responses to literature. He did not regard kindergartners as psychotic, so he removed some of the psychobabble and renamed the steps to sound less experimental. The techniques worked quickly and beautifully, allowing the learners to make profound connections to literature.

Since that time, we have used this revised framework to help learners of all ages become more reflective and thoughtful—from elementary students analyzing difficult poetry to adult leadership teams tackling achievement data.

The 4 *R*s: A Structure for Reflective Conversations

What are the steps of reflective thinking? When adults encounter new information or data, they have a tendency to do one of four things to understand and connect to the information—restate, react, remember, and respond with questions. Though most people do not work through all four of these reflective domains in a linear approach, the 4 *R*s process places them in a metacognitive sequence as presented here. In the vernacular of science, the domains move from observations to hypotheses.

Each stage of reflection has a "timely" connection. Restatement and reactions occur in the present tense. Remembrances are past-tense statements, and responsive questions tend to look toward the future.

Restate: Many learners need to restate information in order to process it. That is, we have to translate information into our own words. Restatements are typically summaries of the information before us. The purpose of this step is to provide clarity and consistency in the interpretation of information. To fully recognize the power of this step of reflection, we must avoid making generalizations or drawing conclusions.

React: Reactions are present-tense (if not knee-jerk) personalized connections to information or data. They allow individuals an opportunity to articulate emotions and thoughts about the data. They range from intensely personal to shared opinions but usually begin with the pronoun *I*. Their purpose is to connect to the information at a personal level.

Remember: The third step of reflective practice is to remember how we experienced something (related to the information or data) in our past. The importance of this step is to provide experiential evidence or concrete examples of a phenomenon.

Respond with questions: This stage of reflection turns our energy toward the future as we ask "What if?" questions or even unanswered "Why?" questions. The purpose of this step is to propose additional connections and considerations or to hypothesize before we jump to conclusions or solve problems.

When we use the four *R*s as a structure to reflect on teaching and learning in a faculty or PLC setting, we follow the steps in order. The first step is processed as a group activity and ends with a written restatement of the situation, information, or data under consideration. A restatement should be a readily agreed-upon truth that anyone can see when looking at the information at hand. The goal of the group's written statement is to come to a consensus about what is in front of them.

Reactions are not written products during the processing of information. Rather, they are oral comments made by individuals in the peer group. Members are asked to read the restatement and then give a short, personalized answer to the question "What do you think about that?" Discussion, interaction, and dialogue are not allowed in this step—each member of the group must take his or her turn reacting to the restatement.

Remembrances are also unwritten. Connecting back to the original information or the restatement of it, each participant shares an anecdote from his or her past as a student. This pushes the focus back on learning rather than teaching. The group may interact during this phase of the process, but each member takes a turn as storyteller.

The final stage ends up in a written product as the peer group captures a list of questions triggered by the data or information considered. Regardless of the intent of individual group members, the questions posed inevitably bring about issues and concerns that the group as a whole must address as it moves forward. In other words, these questions become the basis for developing the next action steps.

Each of the four *R*s has a unique and specific purpose in the reflective process. They each appeal to different motivations, ways of thinking, and even different people. A principal in Idaho once let us know that she intended to omit the third *R*: remember. Her leadership style was fairly straightforward, and she didn't see the need for what she perceived as the "touchy-feely" part of the process. We encouraged her not to short-circuit the process, and she reluctantly agreed. The next time we saw her, she shared this experience with us:

> Well, I hate to admit it, but you were right. I was meeting with my
> 5th and 6th grade team, a group that includes probably my most
> resistant teacher. We were talking about engagement and when we
> got to the third *R*, he shared a story from an undergraduate class.
> He said, "One of my college professors talked and talked and
> talked, and I didn't learn anything." Then he looked at me, his
> expression softened, and he said, "The teacher talked too much."

Since that meeting, the transformation has been amazing. That teacher looks for opportunities to make his content relevant. He does his best to let kids experience things by doing rather than by listening. I didn't think I had time for Remembering, but those few minutes were powerful for the team, the teacher, and his students. We will be doing all four *R*s from now on.

> *Lasting change does not occur without an SEE—significant emotional experience. —Morris Massey*

As noted by the administrator in our previous anecdote, we often do not have time to personalize the objective for adult learners. We work in numerous schools that have incorporated PLCs in an effort to improve learning for their students. With nothing but good intentions, school and district administrators build complex calendars that bring teachers together to reflect and collaborate—often without providing the tools to accomplish either. With no significant emotional experiences, the PLCs then become tiresome exercises of superficial dialogue that do not fundamentally change how the classrooms operate.

Even when PLC members find meaning in the group's discussions, this does not necessarily lead to changes in practice. Another interesting pattern we found in ineffective PLCs is the compliant implementation of a new idea or research-based strategy without thoughtful consideration or analysis. These observations are the basis for our PLC 4 Real model (see Figure 11.2).

The acronym REAL represents the four areas of action that productive PLCs consider as they work to achieve their goals—reflection, experimentation, analysis, and lesson design and redesign.

Reflection: We dedicated an entire chapter of this book to reflection. The shift from teaching to learning cannot occur if we are unable to step back from the role of teacher and place ourselves in the role of learner. In a PLC setting, each group member must have a voice in the process. Without reflection, there can be little change.

Experimentation: Whether it is within a PLC framework or another form of professional development, we find that research and training often do not change practice. It is only through "playing with" the strategy in the safety of

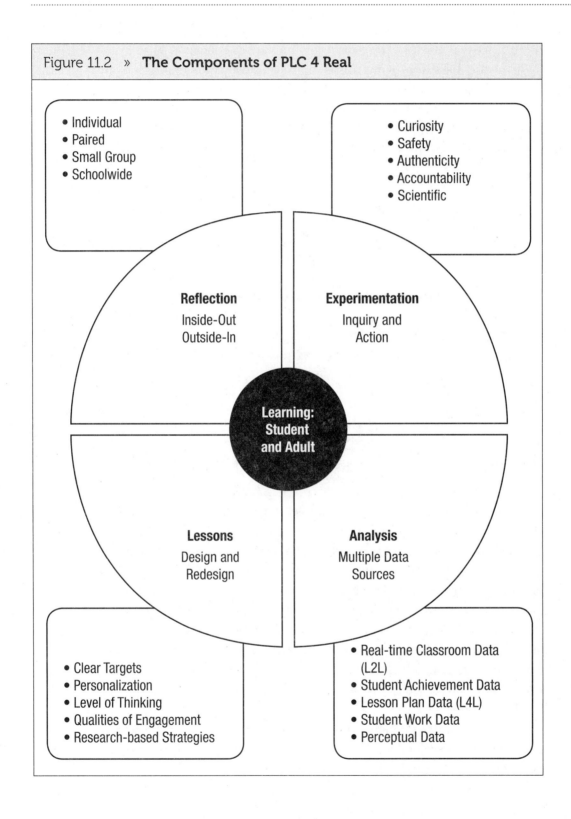

Figure 11.2 » **The Components of PLC 4 Real**

our own classrooms that we can truly determine its effectiveness. In any scientific inquiry, accountability to the results of the experiment is paramount. We must have a plan to measure the success of the trial. If we want to change our practice, then we have to practice the change.

Analysis: In most schools, *data* have become synonymous with test scores. There are, of course, many other sources of data—some much more closely aligned with classroom learning—than test scores. After a classroom experimentation (of a new strategy), analysis of student work might provide the most accurate data. Observational data collected by a peer watching the implementation of a new lesson might be the best way to obtain feedback. Of course, we believe that talking to learners during the learning process contributes the most powerful data of all.

Lesson Design and Redesign: Some popular PLC models spend a considerable amount of time and effort on reteaching and remediation, but collaborative lesson design can lead to more powerful initial instruction—reducing the need for the work of remediation in the PLC. We have come to realize that teachers spend too much time planning their lessons and not enough time designing the learning. We will therefore dig deeper into this distinction in Chapter 12.

The four components of PLC 4 Real constitute neither steps nor a sequence. Rather, they represent a complete process cycle for collaboration. For example, after a district training on a new vocabulary strategy, the PLC work may follow this order:

Experimentation: Each teacher redelivers the example lesson from the training with his or her own classroom of students.
Reflection: At the following PLC meeting, each teacher is asked to share how the implementation worked in his or her classroom.
Analysis: Teachers share student work to determine the success of the lesson and look for patterns and evidence. (e.g., Were all of the students successful? Did English language learners struggle? What was the level of student thinking?)
Lesson Design: Math teachers choose to rework the strategy to make it more meaningful in their current content, and science teachers develop a way to make it more "hands-on."

In Chapter 12, we provide a tool that can help us work through analysis, lesson design, and experimentation. For now, let's end once again on a reflective note.

This chapter had a lot of letters in it: the 4 *R*s, SEE, REAL. Education is awash in acronyms and abbreviations. Why do we love them so much? Perhaps we need acrostics and mnemonic devices to jog our memory—to remind us of that which we want to accomplish. In this case, to remind us of the power of R-E-F-L-E-C-T-I-O-N.

Review the mnemonic in Figure 11.1 (page 152), and consider these questions:

1. Which of the lines resonates most strongly with you? _____

_____

2. Which do you consider to be a personal strength? _____

_____

3. Which might be an area for personal growth? _____

_____

4. Which would be a strength of your school or district? _____

_____

5. Which might be an area of growth for your school or district? _____

_____

Journal:

After two months here at Westside, I keep thinking about the way I used to do things at my old school. Today, I'm sitting in 5th period again and Mr. Rand is talking about World War II. I think I've already done this! He has a great picture of Churchill, Roosevelt and Stalin and he's telling us why it's symbolic. If it's symbolic, I wonder why he doesn't let us figure out the symbolism. (I guess it would take more time.)

In my head, I'm thinking about how you could do a triple venn with lines about the three guys—traits of leadership, connection to regular people, how they motivated, what they believed. I wonder if you could compare Hitler and Mussolini to these good guys at the same time?

I should be writing down the dates from the powerpoint, but I think I'm going to build the world's first PENTabulous venn diagram!

12

Putting It All Together

Although we are approaching the conclusion of this book, it's important to remember what we said in Chapter 10: conclusion doesn't necessarily mean ending. Rather, a conclusion can provide a summary, an outcome, an inference, or a reasoned deduction. So far on our journey together, we've gathered many puzzle pieces: levels of cognition, instructional targets, student engagement, effective strategies, differentiation, closure, and more. Separately, they can seem disjointed or even overwhelming. The purpose of this chapter is to provide structures for classroom implementation that help assemble these pieces in a coherent, satisfying, and practical way.

It is almost impossible to begin a discussion of organizing instruction without referencing the work of Madeline Hunter (1994). Providing one of the first logical and consistent structures for planning a lesson, she developed a seven-step process to help guide teacher decision making.

1. Anticipatory Set: Framing instruction through a short activity or prompt that activates prior knowledge or experience

2. Objective: Selecting and sharing the purpose or relevance of the lesson

3. Input and Modeling: Conveying and demonstrating the vocabulary, skills, and concepts to be learned

4. Checking for Understanding : Observing, interpreting, and evaluating students' grasp of the information presented

5. Guided Practice: Providing students with the opportunity to replicate the teacher's modeling with guidance and support

6. Independent Practice: Releasing students to practice on their own

7. Closure: Summarizing and reviewing the main points of the lesson

The last few steps of this model demonstrate a release of responsibility and control. Hunter once said that the essence of her organizing structure could be expressed in six words: *I do. We do. You do.*

Jim: Madeline Hunter's work certainly was groundbreaking for its time.

John: And yet I'm often surprised by the number of teachers who haven't had the opportunity to experience her ideas.

Jim: Me too—particularly among those who have graduated from college more recently.

John: It is especially troubling because some districts have embedded the model into their planning expectations and even their teacher evaluation instruments.

Jim: Something about which Hunter had some reservations.

John: Yes. She said that all of these elements might not be present every day in every lesson. They were tools to guide and inform teacher decision making and behavior.

Jim: Which, for us, raises an issue with the process. It is very "teaching centered."

John: I'll say! Look at those *–ing* words after each of the seven steps. The teacher is the implied subject for all of them.

Jim: Even her condensed three-stage summary is expressed from the teacher's perspective. I wonder what those three steps would look like if we defined them from the students' point of view.

John: I think we've already said it: connect... do... reflect.

Jim: If we haven't stated it that way, then we've certainly implied it. First, kids have the opportunity to look for relationships between the content and their own knowledge and experiences.

John: Then they participate in activities that lead to learning. Less listening, more doing.

Jim: Finally, they reflect on those activities, identifying the concepts and skills acquired, connecting them to prior learning, and making predictions about the content to come.

John: In fact, one could rewrite the descriptions for each of Hunter's seven steps so they become a model for designing learning experiences rather than a tool for planning teaching.

Jim: I have a great idea! What if, to make that shift complete, we tied the Engaging Qualities to each of the seven steps?

John: I think that's dangerous.

Jim: Why?

John: Well, let's put it this way: I'll only agree to it if you let me put in a disclaimer.

Jim: Oh, good grief.

John: I mean it.

Jim: OK, what do you need to say?

John: The placements of these qualities are only examples of how and where they might occur in a lesson. Each of them can have power at any point in the learning process.

Jim: I'm glad I agreed. That is true and bears emphasizing.

John: So let's look at Madeline Hunter's seven steps with the learning shift in place.

1. *Anticipatory Set:* Students reflect on experiences or participate in atypical activities that will eventually connect to new content. The connection may occur through relevance (Authenticity) or curiosity (Novelty and Variety).

2. *Objective:* Students personalize the lesson's objective through knowledge of what they will experience and why the learning is important to them. They can also articulate how learning will be demonstrated (Clear/Modeled Expectations).

3. *Input and Modeling:* Students participate in activities that will help them define concepts and gain skills. A menu of options may be available for accessing the curriculum (Choice).

4. *Checking for Understanding:* Because they are clear about the desired outcomes, students are able to take an active role in assessing their own progress. For students to be honest and open in sharing this information, they must be comfortable with recognizing and acknowledging mistakes (Intellectual/Emotional Safety).

5. *Guided Practice:* With support and structure, students have the opportunity to demonstrate progress in acquiring skills. This assistance may come from the teacher or fellow students (Learning with Others).

6. *Independent Practice:* With a high degree of content mastery, students practice skills without outside help. Feeling a sense of ownership in the results, the students' level of concern may be heightened (Sense of Audience).

7. *Closure:* Through a brief activity or prompt, students reflect on, summarize, analyze, or prioritize content from the lesson. Closure is a final moment of connection (Personal Response).

This revision of Madeline Hunter's seven-step process may assist us in continuing to define the teaching-learning shift, but perhaps Jerrod can help us take it a step further.

We were recently asked to create the content and structure for an online lesson design protocol. The format needed to incorporate research and best practices, be helpful and intuitive for teachers, and be learning-focused. We decided to look to another successful software product for some guidance— TurboTax. This program takes a very complex process and guides users through it by proposing a series of questions. The questions are presented in an order that is logical to the client but not necessarily the order in which the data will appear on the completed form.

In addition, we borrowed a strategy from the teacher referenced in Chapter 5 and made use of his craft sticks. We thought it most powerful to frame the questions from the learner's point of view, and to ensure that happened, we (figuratively) pulled Jerrod's stick from the can. The results are shown in Figure 12.1. Even though the official title of this tool is Questions for Learner-Focused Lesson Design, we informally refer to it as Jerrod's Questions.

You may notice that the structure doesn't provide a script for teachers to use in the classroom. Rather, it is meant to help shift focus and view the lesson and the acquisition of content and skills from the students' perspective. Put another way, it can help us design learning experiences rather than plan teaching. Although you will find ideas from several bodies of research included, the underlying structure is backward design (Wiggins & McTighe, 2005). Learning targets are identified, assessment methods are described and shared, and activities are selected that will help students successfully reach those goals.

Jerrod's Questions can encourage reflective practice, generate professional conversations, and help us see the lesson through the eyes of the learner. The questions alone are less valuable as a tool for everyday lesson design; much of the heavy lifting in planning—especially in a learning-focused environment— lies in designing rigorous and engaging tasks that will help students access content. Only one of these questions (What activities will help me reach the objective?) addresses that work. To go further and deeper with the *L* of PLC 4 Real—Lesson Design and Redesign—another structure is necessary.

Figure 12.1 » Questions for Learner-Focused Lesson Design

Standard
What do I need to know?

Relevance
Why do I need to know that today?
Why will I need to know that in the future?
What activity, question, or model will grab my attention and frame my thinking?

Objective
What will I be able to do when we're done? (verb)
What will my product or performance look like? (context)
As a student, how well do I need to do it? (criteria)
How will the objective be communicated to me? How will I personalize it?
How will I show you I understand the objective?

Preassessment
How will I show you what I already know about this?

Vocabulary
Are there new words I need to know—either content or process?

Input/Modeling
What activities will help me reach the objective?
How will I show you my progress?

Practice
What will we practice together?
What will I practice alone?

Closure
How will I summarize and reflect on my new learning?

A number of years ago, we were asked to partner with the Green River Regional Educational Cooperative (GRREC), a forward-thinking organization in Bowling Green, Kentucky. This educational service center provides support, training, and leadership to its 35 member school districts in 26 counties across South Central Kentucky. We were asked to extend GRREC's great work on content, coaching, and standards by helping the member districts define and look for cognitive engagement in a year-long training institute entitled *Designing Student Engagement*.

Although the title featured the word *designing*, Associate Executive Director for Learning Services Sandra Baker recognized that the components of engagement would be more tangible and meaningful to her teachers and administrators if we took more of an analytical approach. In other words, instead of providing a template for designing engaging work, she wanted us to first find the components through an analysis of training tasks, student work, classroom videos, and L2L walkthroughs. Sandra wanted us to answer the question "How do we look for engagement?" before answering the question "How do we plan for engagement?"

The six days of training subsequently broke down the idea of engagement into three major components—academic engagement, cognitive/intellectual engagement, and egocentric engagement. After working on the individual components, we introduced a Rubik's Cube as a metaphor to remind teachers that no single component can guarantee engagement for all. Figure 12.2 presents our version of the famous puzzle toy.

Many of us (the authors included) gave up solving the Rubik's Cube years ago when we finally mastered red only to find we had messed up orange. We were frustrated by our inability to see that the trick in solving the Rubik's Cube is to be mindful of the relationships among the colors rather than concentrating on one color at a time. This metaphor served our group well as a reminder of our ultimate goal—"putting it all together."

In a fashion similar to the layout of this book, the GRREC training presented one set of ideas at a time to avoid overwhelming educators who were already working at a frantic pace. With the REAL model of professional collaboration in mind, each teacher's classroom experimentation was analyzed for the power of its engaging components. Combined with reflection, the process ensured that we developed a deep understanding of the components—long before we approached Lesson Design and Redesign.

One of the most important ideas that consistently arose as teachers reflected on the analysis of classroom visits was that it was not always easy to decide if a component was present in the work or not. Participants argued whether "a little bit of personal response" made the activity truly engaging or meaningful. When some students used the strategy of identifying similarities and differences but others did not, was the strategy a real part of the task design or were some kids just taking it to the next level? It soon became apparent to the group that many of the components exist along a continuum. This became an invaluable tool to fully analyze (and evaluate) a design component's impact on learning. (As we have already played with the idea of continua throughout this book, we will not over-explain the tool.)

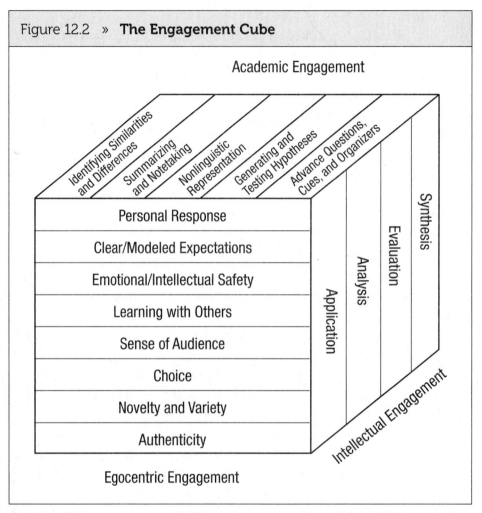

Figure 12.2 » **The Engagement Cube**

Source: From *Writing as a measure and model of thinking: A mira process* (p. 85), by J. V. Antonetti, 2008, Phoenix, AZ: Flying Monkeys Press. Copyright 2008 by Flying Monkeys Press. Reprinted with permission.

To make the Engagement Cube more practical, we reconfigured it into a series of linear continua arranged by "power components," allowing the relationships among them to be even more visual. The Powerful Task Rubric for Designing Student Work shown in Figure 12.3 was the result. With the GRREC teachers, we continued to use this tool for analysis of student work.

Hopefully, the elements of this rubric will be familiar to you from concepts presented earlier in this book. (You may want to keep a finger on Figure 12.3 as you read the rest of this chapter.)

Figure 12.3 » **Powerful Task Rubric for Designing Student Work**

The "Rigor Divide" (between columns 2 and 3)

Category	Power Component	1	2	3	4
Cognitive Demand	Bloom: Revised Taxonomy	Recall	Understand	Apply/Analyze	Evaluate/Create
	Examples	Name the steps	Follow the steps	Infer with text support	Argue, defend, or justify
	Antonetti/Garver: Patterns	Repeat patterns	Restate or reproduce patterns	Find patterns / Find use for patterns	Compare patterns / Add/combine/ignore patterns
	Webb: DOK (Assessment)	Recall	Skill/Concept	Strategic thinking	Extended thinking
	Stein/Smith: Mathematics	Memorization	Procedures without connections	Procedures with connections	Doing Mathematics
Academic Strategies*	Similarities and Differences	List facts about *A* and *B*	Parallel facts about *A* and *B*	Compare or contrast by trait	
	Summarizing/Notetaking	Copy	Restate	Personalize or make unique decisions about content	
	Nonlinguistic Representation	Copy other given forms	Place into other forms	Create a new representation	
	Generating/Testing Hypotheses	Copy	Restate a "known" pattern	Identify and extend patterns	
Engaging Qualities**	Personal Response (Clear/Modeled Expectations)	Not necessary	Fill in the blank with "my" answer	Explain and support my ideas (open)	Explain and defend or justify my ideas
	Intellectual/Emotional Safety	Not required	Not required	Expression of concepts or recognized patterns	Expression of supported opinions or new ideas
	Learning with Others	Take turns talking	Listen and repeat	Interdependence in roles or mini-tasks	Interdependence of ideas
	Sense of Audience	A partner	The class	An audience I want to appreciate me or my ideas	An audience I want to influence
	Novelty and Variety	Recall is fun or different	Product without concepts	Product with concepts	Perspective
	Authenticity	Teacher connects to world	Repeat real examples	Recognize real examples	Create real examples
	Questions	Closed with single right or wrong answers	Closed but with a "choice" of answers	Open with a range of answers, support, strategies, connections	

* The strategies listed are those directly influencing rigor or cognitive demand.
** The engaging quality of Choice is not listed; it is effectively provided through choice between rigorous tasks.

Let's take a moment to revisit Tasks A and B from Chapter 4 and compare them using the Powerful Task Rubric. (To jog your memory—Task A was listing the 50 states and capitals and Task B was determining criteria that would be important to you as you relocate to another state.) Let's start with each of the reflective questions we asked about the tasks and move them into a more analytical approach.

Since question 1 asked which task you enjoyed, we will begin with the component of Engaging Qualities. Most people report that Task B is more enjoyable because they are allowed to think their own thoughts. If we consider the continuum of Personal Response, Task B is described by the Level 3 indicator *explain and support my ideas*. (Is gardening a criterion of climate or of recreation?) If the learner proposes and explains multiple answers but then lands on the better or best "fit," then Personal Response would hit Level 4. When we consider Task A in terms of the same quality, it is clearly a Level 1 task—there is no Personal Response in alphabetizing the states. Everyone's list should always be the same.

Nevertheless, some people find Task A more engaging. Let's consider why that is. People who are competitive may prefer Task A because they want to impress everybody else in the room by quickly reciting the "Nifty Fifty United States" rap and beating the clock. On the continuum for Sense of Audience, the task might be a Level 3. When we perform this activity in groups of teachers, we can almost guess who will win Task A by watching the groups work for the first 30 seconds. The winning teams inevitably break up the task and have one member write states from the beginning (starting with Alabama) while another starts from the end (with Wyoming). Two other teammates fill in the capitals at the same time. On the Learning with Others continuum, *interdependence in roles or mini-tasks* indicates a Level 3 result. (However, this may be a result of the personalities of the group members rather than the design of the work.)

At the same time, the second part of Task B is predicated on Learning with Others since the final product requires each group of participants to combine and categorize ideas guaranteeing an *interdependence of ideas* at a Level 4.

"Which task did you find to be more difficult and why?" was the second question we proposed in Chapter 4. As we said in that chapter, difficulty is in the eye of the learner, not in the task. For that reason, the Powerful Task Rubric does not inspect for difficulty. Rather, it asks us to analyze the cognitive demand of the task using one of a number of cognitive taxonomies, based upon our work or the work of Bloom et al. (1956); Webb (2005); or

Stein, Smith, Henningsen, & Silver (2009). Based on past experiences with the teachers, content area, or language used in a particular district, one of these taxonomies might be more suitable than the others. On the other hand, many teachers move comfortably through the indicators, using more than one taxonomy to anchor their analyses.

Let's get back to Tasks A and B and look at the cognition. Using any of the four taxonomies, see if you can find where Task A lands. As learners list the states in order and remember the capitals, the task falls at Level 1 or Level 2 cognitive demand. If they rely on the song, then the cognition is obviously recall at Level 1. If they pull states off a map and then actually alphabetize them, the cognition is a Level 2—using the skill of alphabetizing. Sadly, a group that finds a website with the states already in order and listed along with their capitals simply copies the list and doesn't even attain the cognition of Level 1.

A sidebar: We have witnessed a number of schools that are proud of their one-to-one technology integration, only to have the technology diminish cognition. It is for this reason that we encourage schools to use the task rubric to determine if technology is enhancing and propelling cognition or at least guaranteeing the desired cognitive demand.

Back to Task B. When the group develops category names for their criteria (e.g., climate, economics, demographics), they are working at Bloom's analysis level. Task B has a cognitive demand of Level 3. If the group is engaged in "best fit" arguments ("The criterion *parks* is more about *community* than *recreation*"), then the cognition moves to *argue, defend, or justify* from Level 4. At a minimum, the task demands a Level 3 of each learner.

Now let's introduce a new question: Which task has rigor? Be careful before you answer—don't let "fun" or "difficulty" cloud your mind. In the many states in which we work, school systems often proclaim, "Let's plan more rigorous instruction!" However, we are often unable to get a working definition of *rigor* from the people who are asking or planning for it. The *Glossary of Educational Reform* (Abbott, 2014) defines rigorous learning experiences as "academically, intellectually, and personally challenging." Note the correlation to the facets of the Engagement Cube—academic engagement, intellectual engagement, and egocentric engagement.

If we may postpone our answer for another moment, let's first consider the remaining component—academic engagement. When we place the academic strategies from Chapter 7 onto the Powerful Task Rubric, the continua look a bit different. Levels 1 and 2 mark a progression toward the inclusion or implementation of an academic strategy. Crossing the double line beyond Level 2 indicates that the strategy was implemented fully. There is no differentiation between a Level 3 and Level 4 strategy.

If we try to place Task A, it does not move beyond Level 1. One could argue that there are no academic strategies used in the alphabetization of states and recall of capitals, yet the closest connection would be to Note Taking—with the matching indicator of *copy* describing the work. When we look at Task B, we can consider a number of strategies that firmly place the task across the double line. The note-taking portion of Task B required each group member to personalize and make unique decisions about content. The group also generated and tested hypotheses as they worked to identify and extend patterns in naming the social studies categories. In terms of similarities and differences, the group's determination of best fit hits the indicator *compare and contrast by trait*.

Now we can return to the idea of rigor. The Powerful Task Rubric incorporates the previously mentioned definition of *rigor* as we look to see if all three power components crossed the Rigor Divide. To be clear, a task is deemed rigorous only when the cognitive demand, academic strategies, and engaging qualities all make it across the double line. A task that has indicators from one or two components across the divide may be rigorous to some learners but not to others. The guarantee of rigor is predicated on all three components adding their respective power to the task. Therefore, Task B crosses the Rigor Divide; Task A does not.

When we consider lesson plans, student work, or classrooms, the rubric becomes a tool to analyze the task at hand. Sadly, if you give a teacher a rubric to apply to his or her own classroom, he or she may want everything to land at Level 3 or 4 and be rigorous. We are, after all, school people, and we want the best numbers, the highest grade, and the gold star. The truth is that many tasks in school should remain at Level 1, and we have to give ourselves permission to make each task match the objective and standard. For example, memorization of multiplication facts is (by definition) a Level 1 task.

When analyzing student tasks and marking where they fall on the rubric, GRREC teachers naturally began to propose "What if?" ideas. They wondered how they could move a Level 2 skill to Level 3 or push Personal Response from *fill in the blank with my answer* across the divide to *explain and support my ideas*. In this way, the tool very quickly became a vehicle for lesson redesign.

In Mrs. Duncan's middle school language arts classroom, we (along with members of her PLC) watched students select a character from Louis Sachar's novel *Holes* and list three character traits. Students then shared their answers with a partner. As we plotted the task on the rubric, the Level 2 indicators described the student work. Later, in the English PLC, Mrs. Duncan and her colleagues reflected on the student work and agreed that Level 2 was the correct analysis. Mrs. Duncan said she would like to add something "from the other side of the divide to make the task better." An exciting brainstorming session followed as many ideas were proposed to make the task more powerful.

Side note: the word *better* implies that the original task was not good. Likewise, the phrase *more powerful* may imply that the original task was weak or not of value. For that reason, we do not use comparative terms when modeling this process. Rather, we talk about adding something from the other side of the divide or proposing a "plus 1" to the original task.

When the discussion ended, the task had been redesigned and was delivered the next day. As we describe what we saw 24 hours later, see if you can find which indicators were added. In this case, the "plus 1" became "plus many."

Students were placed in groups of three, each taking a different character from the story. They repeated the first assignment of listing three character traits. Then the groups were asked to identify scenes in which one character's trait interacted with a second character's trait and thereby explained the plot point, dialogue, or scene.

One group of students was having this dialogue:

"Well, I have that Stanley is bullied and is a bully to Zero, is unsure of himself, but is kind of positive and doesn't get depressed."

"I have that Zero was kind and giving. Do you have anything that goes with that?"

"Well, what about when Zero gives Stanley his last jar of 'Sploosh'? It helps Stanley with his self-confidence."

"It also stops him from bullying Zero."

"That's a good one. Write that one down."

"Ok, my turn. I have that X-ray is nice, jealous, and smart."

"Oooh, X-ray is nice to Stanley when Stanley is bullying Zero, but when those two become friends, X-ray gets jealous and shuts Stanley out."

We began to notice some powerful trends in schools that used the Powerful Task Rubric for the *plus 1* redesign. Students became more thoughtful in their responses, taking ownership of their ideas and the evidence to support them.

The frequency of worksheets decreased. Kids who had previously shied away from responding became more verbal and more confident in their thinking and problem solving. Students were grasping concepts quicker and to a greater depth. The learners and the teachers reported that they were enjoying the lessons more and that the learning was more fun. A final result: standardized test scores went up.

"Give the pupils something to do, not something to learn. . . . [If] the doing is of such a nature to demand thinking, learning naturally results." —John Dewey

Ultimately, the Powerful Task Rubric for Designing Student Work should become the tool its name suggests—a protocol for lesson design. When we were students, most of us were not taught to the higher levels of rigor, and even fewer of us were taught to design such activities as preservice teachers. Therefore, we believe the rubric should be used in collaborative settings when approaching lesson design rather than by individual teachers.

We also believe that rigor is most readily designed from the cognitive verb in the standard or objective. Unfortunately, some standards possess rather "empty" verbs such as *list, write,* and *describe,* which do not appropriately identify the cognitive demand. (Thinking back to the cognition required in Tasks A and B, it is interesting to note that the first verb in both activities was *list.*) In the case of weak verbs, the PLC must discern the intended cognitive level.

To illustrate the beginning of the design process, let us dissect a high school example from the Next Generation Science Standards:

HS-PS1-1: Use the periodic table as a model to predict the relative properties of elements based on the patterns of electrons in the outermost energy level of atoms. (National Research Council, 2013)

When we dissect this standard, we find the student verbs *use* and *predict.* The cognitive verb—*predict*—is where we will begin to design for rigor. As a first step in the process, we would typically ask the PLC to try to define the verb or articulate the steps of the cognitive verb, free of the other content in the standard. Put simply, what does predicting entail? How does one predict?

If we think about prediction as a cognitive process, the final step is to guess what comes next or what will happen in the future. Prior to that, the brain must look at some information and determine what patterns or trends are present. In street terms, there are three steps:

1. Look at something.
2. Figure out what is going on.
3. Decide what might happen next.

After playing with the cognitive verb a bit, the PLC members are asked to find the most obvious or likely connections between the verb and the indicators on the Powerful Task Rubric. Please note that we are not talking about the nouns of content yet—just the verbs.

The team proposes that prediction connects in Cognitive Demand with *infer with text support, find patterns, find use for patterns,* and *analyze.* Other members may jump to the indicator *identify and extend patterns* from the Academic Strategies. These indicators purport that the standard requires crossing the rigor divide in at least two of the power components.

Even if the design discussion ends now, we have already had an important moment in shifting from teaching to learning. If a teacher teaches the periodic trends by showing students what is going on with electron patterns in the periodic table, the student action of *predicting* does not include the second step, and the learning task is reduced to Level 2 at best. The task would be characterized by the indicators of *follows the steps, restates or reproduces patterns,* and *procedures without connections.*

As the task design process continues, the PLC decides they want to push toward the rigor guarantee by adding Engaging Qualities of Level 3 or 4. One member suggests having students work interdependently, and another proposes some sort of Intellectual/Emotional Safety element. A third member thinks having students compare multiple versions of the periodic table might lead to increased analysis and a personal response. The brainstorming aspect of this teacher-to-teacher dialogue is perhaps the most important part of the design process. Most teachers already have activities in mind for teaching a particular concept. By starting from scratch with the standard and the Powerful Task Rubric, we could say that we are practicing lesson design, but in reality we may just be rethinking an activity from our past and redesigning it before ever presenting it to the learners.

Once again, the goal is to shift from teaching to learning.

When we work with educators, we sometimes propose the question "Are kids today different from when you were in school?" As we said earlier, the consensus is usually that they are. Occasionally, someone will propose that kids' motivations are similar, but the environment is different. Regardless, the implications are obvious and profound. If our students (or the world in which they live) have undergone significant changes, how have we modified our organization and professional practices to meet the changing needs of our clients? We hope the content of this chapter—and this book—has provided you with reflection, tools, and strategies to help frame your response.

Think about a lesson you recently taught. (If you are not currently in the classroom, think about a lesson you observed.)

The closure for this chapter will provide you with the opportunity for choice. You may opt for either of the following activities:

1. Using the content from the lesson you identified, answer the Questions for Learner-Focused Lesson Design. In light of this new perspective, how might you plan instruction differently? *(Reflection, Lesson Design)*

2. Determine the critical learning activity in the lesson you identified and plot its components on the Powerful Task Rubric. How might you move any Level 1s and 2s across the Rigor Divide? *(Analysis, Lesson Redesign)*

So long 7th grade! I'm sitting on the bus going home on the last day and it is over forever!

Dad said in honor of my great year, I could have his old iPad since his company is giving him a new one. I can't decide if I'll keep writing in this new journal or just start my own 8th grade blog.

I can't believe how mad I was when Mrs. G. made us do this on the first day of the year. She was pretty smart. Actually they all were—Garcia, Hansen, Lee (but not Diemer the Dud sub!). I didn't realize how good my teachers were until I got to Lincoln. My new teachers were nice and all. I guess they were good teachers—they know a lot of stuff—they just didn't know how to make me want to learn it.

Oh well. There's always next year!

13

Final Thoughts

John: Well, it looks like we've come to the end of the book.

Jim: And, in the writing, what a long but enjoyable journey it's been. A little strange sometimes, but definitely enjoyable.

John: I'm glad you used the word *journey*. In many ways, this book describes our journey and the evolution of our thoughts over the past decade while visiting these various and varied classrooms.

Jim: I sometimes worry that when people see the data from our walks, they will be discouraged or even angry.

John: I worry about that, too. But I hope they understand that we are merely recording what we see. The perspective changes dramatically when we look at the lesson through the lens of the learner.

Jim: Wow, that's almost a tongue twister! But I like it. I also hope folks understand that we didn't model each and every one of these things in our own classrooms when we were teaching.

John: Not consistently, anyway. We didn't know what we do now.

Jim: But if we now have that new knowledge, as professionals, don't we have an obligation to apply it?

John: In the medical profession, the answer would certainly be *yes*. And I think we see great examples of successful application in the partner schools with whom we work.

Jim: The L2L data would certainly bear that out. We see upward trends in many of those schools and districts.

John: What do you think they have in common?

Jim: Well, one thing is strong leadership. We see vision, resources, and authority concentrated—or at least coordinated—to guide professional development.

John: And teacher leaders are frequently part of the equation.

Jim: I would agree. What do you see?

John: Those successful schools and districts give their teachers the gift of time—time to train, time to plan, time to collaborate, time to analyze data, time to experiment, and time to reflect.

Jim: That's a lot of time!

John: But all of it is crucial to growth and changes in practice. What else do you see in those successful schools?

Jim: Focus. They are not trying to implement the staff development flavor of the month. As part of that focus, they also provide opportunities to explore connections between and among initiatives. "We worked on thinking levels a couple of years ago. How do our current efforts to enhance engagement relate to that?"

John: The brain does look for patterns and relationships. Successful schools and districts also give things time to work. They look for long-term improvement and use sources of data (such as Look 2 Learning) to identify benchmarks for success.

Jim: So: time, focus, and time.

John: Seems a bit redundant, but we've seen it work.

Jim: Well, we've almost reached the back cover. I guess that means we're done.

John: No, like all thoughtful professionals, we'll never be done. The learning goes on.

Jim: Does that apply to our readers, too?

John: I certainly hope so.

Jim: Can we say something directly to them now?

John: I think we have been. What would you like to say?

Jim: We've enjoyed having you along for the journey.

John: I would add that we hope to cross paths during our travels. And I'm sure we both want to say...

Both: Thank you.

References

Abbott, S. E. (Ed.). (2014, February 11). *Glossary of Educational Reform* [Scholarly project]. Retrieved June 18, 2014, from http://edglossary.org/rigor/

Antonetti, J. V. (2008). *Writing as a measure and model of thinking: A mira process.* Phoenix, AZ: Flying Monkeys Press.

Asher, J. J., & Adamski, C. (2009). *Learning another language through actions.* Los Gatos, CA: Sky Oaks Productions.

Bender, W. N., & Shores, C. (2007). *Response to intervention: A practical guide for every teacher.* Arlington, VA: Council for Exceptional Children.

Bloom, B. S. (1956). *Taxonomy of educational objectives: The classification of educational goals.* New York: McKay.

Dean, C. B., Hubbell, E. R., Pitler, H., & Stone, B. (2012). *Classroom instruction that works* (2nd Ed.). Alexandria, VA: ASCD.

Dewey, J. (1933). *How we think: A restatement of the relation of reflective thinking to the educative process.* Boston: DC Heath.

DuFour, R., DuFour, R. B., & Eaker, R. E. (2008). *Revisiting professional learning communities at work: New insights for improving schools.* Bloomington, IN: Solution Tree.

Enterprise Media (Producer). (2006). *What you are is where you were when...again! with Morris Massey.* [DVD]. Cambridge, MA: Enterprise Media.

Fisher, D., & Frey, N. (2007). *Checking for understanding: Formative assessment techniques for your classroom.* Alexandria, VA: ASCD.

Gardner, H. (2006). *Multiple intelligences: New horizons.* New York: BasicBooks.

Hunter, M. C. (1994). *Mastery teaching.* Thousand Oaks, CA: Corwin.

Jensen, E. (2005). *Teaching with the brain in mind.* Alexandria, VA: ASCD.

Maslow, A. H. (1993). *The farther reaches of human nature.* New York: Arkana.

Medina, J. (2008). *Brain rules: 12 principles for surviving and thriving at work, home, and school.* Seattle, WA: Pear Press.

Meyer, D. (2013, August 1). Math class needs a makeover - Dan Meyer. Retrieved from https://www.youtube.com/watch?v=qocAoN4jNwc

National Research Council (2013). *Next generation science standards: For states, by states.* Washington, DC: The National Academies Press.

Parkes, B., Smith, J., & Davy, M. (1986). *The enormous watermelon.* Melbourne, Australia: Maurbern Pty.

Payne, R. K. (2013). *A framework for understanding poverty: A cognitive approach* (5th ed.). Highlands, TX: Aha! Process.

Pink, D. H. (2011). *Drive: The surprising truth about what motivates us*. New York: Riverhead Books.

Schlechty, P. C. (2002). *Working on the work: An action plan for teachers, principals, and superintendents*. San Francisco: Jossey-Bass.

Small, M. (2012). *Good questions: Great ways to differentiate mathematics instruction*. New York: Teachers College Press.

Smith, M. S., & Stein, M. K. (1998). Selecting and creating mathematical tasks: from research to practice. *Mathematics in the Middle School, 3(5): 348.*

Stein, M., Smith, M., Henningsen, M., & Silver, E. (2009). *Implementing standards-based mathematics instruction: A casebook for professional development*. Reston, VA: National Council of Teachers of Mathematics.

Stiggins, R. (2007). Assessment through the student's eyes. *Educational Leadership, 64(8),* 22–26.

Stigler, J. W., & Hiebert, J. (2004). Improving mathematics teaching. *Educational Leadership, 61(5),* 12–17.

Tomlinson, C. A. (2014). *The differentiated classroom: Responding to the needs of all learners* (2nd Ed.). Alexandria, VA: ASCD.

Webb, N. L. (2005, November 15). *Alignment, depth of knowledge, & change* [Scholarly project]. Retrieved from http://facstaff.wcer.wisc.edu/normw/miami%20florida%20final%20slides%2011-15-05.pdf

Wiggins, G., & McTighe, J. (2005). *Understanding by design (expanded 2nd Ed.)*. Alexandria, VA: ASCD.

Wolf, P., & Supon. V. (1994). *Winning through student participation in lesson closure*. Bloomsburg, PA: Bloomsburg University. (ERIC Document Reproduction Service No. ED 368 694)

York-Barr, J., Sommers, W. A., Ghere, G. S., & Montie, J. (2001). *Reflective practice to improve schools: An action guide for educators*. Thousand Oaks, CA: Corwin.

Index

The letter *f* following a page number denotes a figure.

About the Authors

In 2006, John Antonetti and Jim Garver formed Colleagues on Call, an educational services company that provides training and consulting to schools and districts across North America. They have worked in 38 U.S. states and five Canadian provinces and territories. Together, they have created Look 2 Learning, a learner-focused walkthough protocol; Lessons 4 Learning, an online program for designing instruction; and PLC 4 Real, a framework for effective collaboration. John and Jim are coauthors of *Focus on Learning*, which provides a process for personal and shared reflection.

John can be reached at info@411oncall.com.

 **John Antonetti** is the former director of K–12 curriculum in the Sheridan School District, Arkansas. Once described by Larry Lezotte as a "teacher's teacher," John has had the great fortune to teach at all grade levels. He has taught kindergarten, AP Chemistry, and most grades in between. He has worked with three districts that won the nationally recognized Broad Prize for Urban Education. He works with schools and districts throughout North America on student engagement, writing, rigor and relevance, and high-yield best practices. Though hands-on work in schools is his passion, John is also a highly sought keynote speaker. His humor and parables are recognized by teachers, administrators, and parents as relevant examples of the power of teachers.

John is the author of the book *Writing as a Measure and Model of Thinking*, which provides practical tools to increase student thinking in all subject areas.

Dr. Jim Garver has experience at all levels of public education—from teacher to associate superintendent, kindergarten through high school, small schools to large. Student achievement has increased in every school and district in which Jim has held a leadership position.

Jim works with schools across the country, sharing expertise on classroom walkthroughs, student engagement, instructional leadership, and professional learning communities. One of these schools was recently named a National Title I Distinguished School. At the district level, he provides assistance with strategic planning, community relations, team building, and executive coaching.

Jim's book *The 10 Secrets of Higher Student Achievement* serves as a blueprint for school improvement in several states. He is also the author of *Coaching for Achievement*, a coaching model to provide practical tools for teachers and their leaders.

Related ASCD Resources

At the time of publication, the following ASCD resources were available (ASCD stock numbers appear in parentheses). For up-to-date information about ASCD resources, go to www.ascd.org. You can search the complete archives of *Educational Leadership* at http://www.ascd.org/el.

ASCD Edge™

Exchange ideas and connect with other educators on the social networking site ASCD Edge at http://ascdedge.ascd.org/

Print Products

Better Learning Through Structured Teaching: A Framework for the Gradual Release of Responsibility (2nd Ed.) by Douglas Fisher and Nancy Frey (#113006)

Classroom Instruction That Works: Research-Based Strategies for Increasing Student Achievement, 2nd Edition by Ceri B. Dean, Elizabeth Ross Hubbell, Howard Pitler, and Bj Stone (#111001)

The Differentiated Classroom: Responding to the Needs of All Learners (2nd Ed.) by Carol Ann Tomlinson (#108029)

Engaging Teachers in Classroom Walkthroughs by Donald S. Kachur, Judith A. Stout, and Claudia L. Edwards (#113024)

Formative Classroom Walkthroughs: How Principals and Teachers Collaborate to Raise Student Achievement by Connie M. Moss and Susan M. Brookhart (#115003)

ᴛʜᴇWHOLE CHILD ASCD's Whole Child approach helps schools and communities create learning environments that allow students to be healthy, safe, engaged, supported, and challenged. To learn more about other books and resources that relate to the whole child, visit www.wholechildeducation. org.

For more information: send e-mail to member@ascd.org; call 1-800-933-2723 or 703-578-9600, press 2; send a fax to 703-575-5400; or write to Information Services, ASCD, 1703 N. Beauregard St., Alexandria, VA 22311-1714 USA.